Instructor's Manual

for

Pinel
Biopsychology
Fourth Edition

Prepared by

Michael J. Mana
Western Washington University

Allyn and Bacon
Boston London Toronto Sydney Tokyo Singapore

Copyright © 2000 by Allyn & Bacon
A Pearson Education Company
160 Gould Street
Needham Heights, Massachusetts 02494

Internet: www.abacon.com

ISBN 0-205-29815-X

Printed in the United States of America

10 9 8 7 6 5 4 3 2 1   04 03 02 01 00 99

Table of Contents

PREFACE

HOW TO USE THIS INSTRUCTOR'S MANUAL

I hope that the lecture notes contained in this Instructor's Manual prove useful in your classroom presentation of the material that is contained in BIOPSYCHOLOGY. Each chapter in BIOPSYCHOLOGY is represented by 2 or 3 lectures that capture the key points of the chapter. It would be presumptuous to offer these lecture notes as a definitive source of lecture material for each chapter of BIOPSYCHOLOGY; the subject material is too broad, and my own biases inevitably crept in! With this caveat in mind, I urge you to use the lectures contained in this Instructor's Manual as a skeleton for your own lectures...but make the clothes your own by adding your own anecdotes, personal experiences, research interests and biopsychology trivia! To this end, I have made it possible to obtain a floppy disk that contains all of the lectures in this Instructor's Manual. To receive a copy, contact your local Allyn & Bacon representative and ask for the floppy disk to support BIOPSYCHOLOGY'S Instructor's Manual.

INTEGRATION WITH OTHER *BIOPSYCHOLOGY* ANCILLARIES.

Each set of lecture notes in this Instructor's Manual is cross-referenced to two other valuable resources that accompany BIOPSYCHOLOGY:

1) The BIOPSYCHOLOGY web site at *http://www.abacon.com/pinel*. At this website, you will find over 300 links to sites relevant to the material contained in each chapter of BIOPSYCHOLOGY. Some of these links are included at the end of each set of lecture notes in the Instructor's Manual; however, there are many more links available at the website, and these will be regularly updated and expanded. The website will also contain a *"Hot Topics"* forum which will focus on news about the cutting edge of Biopsychology, a question-and-answer forum for students and faculty, and a *"Interested in Technology?"* forum for faculty where tips and tricks for making the most of the ancillaries for BIOPSYCHOLOGY will be presented.

2) The *Digital Image Archive CD-ROM* for BIOPSYCHOLOGY, available upon request from your Allyn and Bacon representative. To find the figures on the CD-ROM, look in Pinel/Images/BMP for a directory containing images from each chapter. Note that the numbering of the figures in the fourth edition of BIOPSYCHOLOGY do not match with the indexing for the figures on the CD-ROM; to make your life easier, the lecture notes in the Instructor's Manual refer to the appropriate file names from the CD-ROM. If you are blessed with a multi-media classroom, you can display the figures directly from the CD-ROM (this type of presentation will also work with many of the links available at the BIOPSYCHOLOGY website). If you are using more conventional teaching resources, you can print the figures from the *Digital Image Archive* onto overheads; check out the *"Interested in Technology"* section of the website for more information.

In addition to these pedagogical aids, Allyn and Bacon offers a video that illustrates many of the topics covered in BIOPSYCHOLOGY. The Video for Biological Psychology contains short video segments garnered from Films for the Humanities and Sciences; each video segments cover such topics as: anatomy of the brain, DNA, genetics, neurotransmitters, how drugs influence electric impulses in the brain, methods of studying the brain, brain damage, the senses, eating, hormones, sleep, drug addiction, memory, and neuroplasticity. The video segments will help students better understand the workings of the brain and will help foster classroom discussion. This video is available upon request from your Allyn and Bacon representative.

If you have any questions or comments, you can contact me through the website, or at MIKE.MANA@WWU.EDU. Be Well!

Lecture 1a

BIOPSYCHOLOGY: A DIVISION OF NEUROSCIENCE

Outline

1. **A Personal Introduction**

    a. Training and Teaching Experience
    b. Research Interests
    c. Teaching Assistant
    d. Availability of Instructor (and Teaching Assistant)

2. **Organization of The Course**

    a. Text and Ancillary Materials
    b. Lecture Format
    c. Examination Format
    d. Major Assignments
    e. Final Grades

3. **What is Biopsychology?**

    a. study of biological bases of behavior
    b. young discipline
    c. characterized by an eclectic approach

4. **Biopsychology as a Discipline of Neuroscience**

    a. What is Neuroscience?
    b. Biopsychology as a part of Neuroscience

5. **The Diversity of Biopsychological Research**

    a. Human and Nonhuman Subjects
    b. Experiments, Quasiexperimental Studies, and Case Studies
    c. Pure and Applied Research

Lecture Notes

1. **A Personal Introduction...**

    - in order to put lend this course a personal perspective, let me tell you a bit about myself.

    a. Training and Teaching Experience

    - how I first became interested in biopsychology (personal anecdote)
    - undergraduate training
    - graduate training
    - postgraduate experience
    - courses currently teaching

    b. Research Experience

- thesis research
- current research interests
- past research

c. **Teaching Assistant (if possible, have the TA speak about themselves)**

- training
- current research interests

d. **Availability of Instructor and Teaching Assistant**

- office hours and location
- phone numbers/e-mail addresses/web pages

2. **Organization of The Course...What You and I Can Expect!**

a. **Who is The Course For?**

- describe any prerequisites for the course (e.g., Introductory Psychology; Introductory Biology)

b. **Text and Ancillary Materials**

- BIOPSYCHOLOGY by John P.J. Pinel
- STUDY GUIDE for BIOPSYCHOLOGY by Michael J. Mana and John P.J. Pinel
- BIOPSYCHOLOGY WEB SITE at: http://www.abacon.com/pinel (includes a forum for asking Mike Mana questions related to BIOPSYCHOLOGY)
- other assigned reading material

c. **Lecture Format**

- relation of lectures to text
- each lecture will begin with an outline
- questions or comments are encouraged

d. **Examination Format**

- examination dates and content
- nature of final exam (comprehensive or for last block of material?)
- nature of questions
- how grades will be reported; grade cutoffs
- what to do if you think your examination has been incorrectly graded

e. **Major Assignments**

- what are they; when are they due?

f. **Special Learning or Examination Requirements**

- provide information about your institution's learning resource center

g. **Missed Examination or Assignment Policy**

h. **Final Grades**

- how the final grades will be computed

3. **What is Biopsychology?**

- <u>brain</u> and <u>behavior</u> are two of the most interesting subjects of scientific research; <u>b</u>iopsychology focuses on the relation between them

- biopsychologists study how the brain and the rest of the nervous system determine what we perceive, feel, think, say, and do

- a biopsychologist uses an eclectic combination of theories and research from many different areas (e.g., psychology, biology, physiology, pharmacology and anatomy) to better describe, understand and predict behavior

4. **Biopsychology as a Discipline of Neuroscience**

   - until middle of the last century, the brain was studied primarily by philosophers; since then, it has been subjected more and more to scientific study.

   - <u>neuroscience</u> is the study of the nervous system; neuroscience includes many different approaches including <u>neuroanatomy</u>, <u>neurophysiology</u>, <u>neurochemistry</u>, neuroendocrinology, <u>neuropharmacology</u>, and <u>neuropathology.</u>

   - <u>biopsychology</u> is characterized as the discipline of neuroscience that attempts to integrated these various approaches to the study of the nervous system; biopsychologists try to discover how the various neural phenomena studied by neurophysiologists, neuropharmacologists, neuroanatomists etc. relate to one another to produce psychological phenomena such as learning, memory, motivation, and perception; in this way, biopsychology can be viewed as bridge between the disciplines of psychology and neuroscience.

   - the first part of the course will examine the fundamentals of neuroanatomy, neurophysiology, neuropharmacology, genetics, and evolution; the rest of the course will focus on how these biological fundamentals are applied to the study of biopsychological phenomena.

5. **The Diversity of Biopsychological Research: An Eclectic Approach**

   - biopsychologists use a variety of research approaches in their studies; to understand what biopsychology is, you must understand what biopsychologists do

   - this diversity can be illustrated by discussing three dimensions along which biopsychological research varies:

   a) human vs. nonhuman subjects; b) experiments vs. nonexperimental studies; and c) applied vs. pure research

   a. **Human and Nonhuman Subjects**

      <u>A</u>dvantages of human subjects:

      - experimenters can have better (more complete) control during experiments
      - they can follow directions
      - they can report subjective experiences
      - they are often less expensive
      - they have a human brain

      <u>A</u>dvantages of nonhuman subjects:

      - they have more simple nervous systems
      - studying various species makes it possible to use the <u>comparative approach</u>
      - there are fewer ethical constraints (although the ethics of both human and animal research is carefully scrutinized by independent committees)

   b. **Experiments, Quasiexperimental Studies, and Case Studies**

Experiments

- the experiment is the method used by scientists to determine cause and effect relationships
- *Independent Variables*: are set or manipulated by the experimenter; these manipulations produce the different treatment conditions in an experiment
- *Dependent Variables:* reflect the subject's behavior; this is what the experimenter measures
- for each experimental hypothesis there must be only one difference between the various treatment conditions of the experiment (i.e., the independent variable) so that there is only one possible explanation for any effect on the dependent variable: "the independent variable caused it"
- usually a different group of subjects is tested under each treatment condition of the experiment; this is a *between-subjects design*
- in some cases, each subject is tested under each treatment condition of the experiment; this is a *within-subject design*
- the experimenter tries to conduct the experiment in such a way that the independent variable is the only thing that varies between each treatment condition
- the experimenter measures the effect of the independent variable on the dependent variable
- in a well-designed experiment, the experimenter can conclude that any differences in the dependent variable between the various treatment conditions were <u>caused</u> by the independent variable (it's the only possibility)
- although the principle of good experimentation is conceptually simple, it is often difficult in practice to make sure that there is only one difference among conditions; other unintended differences among conditions that can influence the dependent variable are called *confounded variables.*
- the presence of confounded variables makes experiments difficult to interpret because it is impossible to tell how much (if any) of the effect on the dependent variable was caused by the independent variable and how much (if any) was caused by the confounded variable
- an example of a well-designed experiment is the experiment of Lester and Gorzalka (1988) on the <u>Coolidge effect</u> in female hamsters

Quasiexperimental Studies

- sometimes it is not possible to conduct controlled experiments; e.g., if the research involves human subjects, it is often impossible for ethical or technical reasons to assign them to particular conditions and to administer the conditions; instead, researchers must examine subjects in real world situations, using subjects who have self-selected into specific conditions or have, in a sense, already assigned themselves
- the major shortcoming of a quasiexperimental study is that although it can tell the researcher what is related to what (e.g., alcohol consumption is related to brain damage), a quasiexperimental study cannot allow for the control of confounding variables and therefore does not allow a researcher to establish direct cause and effect relationships
- for example, it is not possible to randomly assign humans to control and alcohol groups, and then expose one group to 10 years of alcohol exposure to see if alcohol causes brain damage; instead a researcher must compare alcoholics and nonalcoholics in the real world. This is a classic <u>quasiexperimental study</u>.
- the problem is that because subjects in the real world do not assign themselves to groups randomly, there are inevitably many other differences among the groups that could contribute to differences in the dependent measures. For example, alcoholics have far more brain damage than nonalcoholics; however, it is not clear to what extent alcohol directly causes this difference because alcoholics differ from nonalcoholics in many ways unrelated to their alchohol consumption (e.g., diet; other drug use).

Case Studies

- case studies are scientific studies that focus on a single subject; for example, you will learn later in the course about how the in-depth study of one amnesic subject (H.M.) has contributed much to our understanding of the neural basis of memory
- the main problem with case studies is their *generalizability,* or the extent to which their results tell us something about the general population.

A Key Point: Experiments, quasiexperimental studies, and case studies can all make valuable scientific contributions, particularly when they are used to complement one another (e.g., they have all contributed to our understanding of the relation between alcohol consumption and brain damage).

c. **Pure and Applied Research**

- pure and applied research are defined by the motivation of the researcher
- pure research is motivated primarily by the curiosity of the researcher; it is motivated by the desire to find out how things work; pure research focuses on establishing building blocks or basic concepts that may provide information salient to many problems
- applied research is motivated by an attempt to directly use the building blocks of basic research to answer specific questions; human and animal problems are directly addressed

Closing Comments:

- biopsychologists study the biology of behavior in a variety of ways; the strength of biopsychology as a science is attributable to this diversity; its diversity also makes biopsychology an exciting and challenging field of study; there is much in this course that will interest and excite you

Suggested Web Resources for Lecture 1a:

Biopsychology and the Nobel Prize: *http://weber.u.washington.edu/~chudler/nobel.html*

List of Noble Prize winners from the behavioral and brain sciences.

A Timeline of Neuroscience: *http://neurolab.jsc.nasa.gov/timeline.htm*

From NASA's Neurolab, a time-line on the history of neuroscience.

The Society for Neuroscience: *http://www.sfn.org*

Homepage for the Society for Neuroscience.

The American Psychological Association: *http://www.apa.org*

Homepage for the APA.

The American Psychological Society: *http://www.psychologicalscience.org*

Homepage for the APS.

The concepts of science, in all their richness and ambiguity,
can be presented without any compromise...
in language accessible to all intelligent people.

Stephen Jay Gould

Lecture 1b

BIOPSYCHOLOGICAL RESEARCH

Outline

1. **Summary of Preceding Lecture**

2. **The Six Divisions of Biopsychology**

   a. Physiological Psychology
   b. Psychopharmacology
   c. Neuropsychology
   d. Psychophysiology
   e. Cognitive Neuroscience
   f. Comparative Psychology

3. **How Biopsychologists Study the Unobservable**

   a. the scientific method and scientific inference

4. **Converging Operations**

   a. biopsychological research integrates information from several different approaches

5. **Two Examples of BS...(Bad Science)**

   a. Taming a Charging Bull with Brain Stimulation
   b. Prefrontal Lobotomy

6. **Class Discussion**

   a. What was wrong with Delgado's claims?
   b. What was wrong with Moniz's claims?

Lecture Notes

1. **Brief Summary of Preceding Lecture**

   - biopsychology is a part of neuroscience
   - biopsychological research is diverse:
     - human and nonhuman subjects
     - experiments, quasiexperimental studies, and case studies
     - pure and applied research

2. **The Six Divisions of Biopsychology**

   a. **Physiological Psychology**

      - focuses on direct manipulation of the nervous system in controlled laboratory settings (e.g., lesions, electrical stimulation, invasive recording)
      - thus, the subjects are usually laboratory animals
      - strong focus on pure research

b. **Psychopharmacology**

- similar to physiological psychology except that the nervous system is manipulated pharmacologically
- focuses on drug effects on behavior and how changes are mediated by changes in neural activity
- many psychopharmacologists favor pure research and use drugs to reveal the nature of brain-behavior interactions; many others study applied questions (e.g., drug abuse, therapeutic drugs)

c. **Neuropsychology**

- focuses on the behavioral deficits produced in humans by brain damage
- can't be studied in humans by experimentation; deals almost exclusively with case studies and quasiexperimental studies
- most applied of the six divisions of biopsychology; neuropsychological tests of brain-damaged patients facilitate diagnosis, treatment, and lifestyle counseling (e.g., the case of Mr. R, p. 10 of text)

d. **Psychophysiology**

- focuses on the relation between physiology and behavior by recording the physiological responses of human subjects
- because human subjects are used, all brain recording is noninvasive (i.e., from the surface of the head)
- usual measure of brain activity is the scalp electroencephalogram (EEG)
- muscle tension, eye movement, heart rate, pupil dilation, and electrical conductance of the skin are other common psychophysiological measures

e. **Cognitive Neuroscience**

- newest division of biopsychology
- focuses on the neural bases of cognitive processes like learning and memory, attention, and complex perceptual processes.
- often employs human subjects; key methods are noninvasive, functional brain imaging techniques

f. **Comparative Psychology**

- study of evolutionary and genetic factors in behavior
- features comparative and functional approaches
- features laboratory research as well as studies of animals in their natural environments (ethology)

3. **How Biopsychologists Study the Unobservable**

- science is a method of answering questions by direct observation; it is an empirical method
- however, brain activity is not directly observable (e.g., one can't see a neuron firing or neurochemicals being released from neurons)
- this situation is no different than that in the other sciences; e.g., physicists cannot see gravity, chemists cannot see evaporation; the effects of these processes are observable but not the processes themselves

   Question: *How do scientists study the unobservable by a method (i.e., the scientific method) that is fundamentally observational?*

   Answer: *By scientific inference; scientists observe the consequences of unobservable processes and from these they infer the nature of unobservable processes.*

- When you consider that scientific inference is the same procedure used by detectives to solve unwitnessed crimes, by treasure hunters to determine the location of sunken galleons from archival documents, and by skilled bridge players to deduce who is holding the lone unplayed trump card, you can appreciate why a career in research is so much fun!

4. Converging Operations

-   the methods of the six divisions of biopsychology are not without their weaknesses; thus, biopsychological issues are rarely resolved by a single experiment or study, or by a single approach
-   progress is greatest when several different approaches, each compensating for the shortcomings of the others, are used to solve the same problems
-   this is called ***converging operations***; this is an extremely important concept and one of the major themes of this course

    Example: Consider the relative strengths and weakness of physiological psychology and neuropsychology in studying the function of the human cortex. Neuropsychology's strength is that it deals with humans, but this is also its weakness because it precludes experimentation. In contrast, physiological psychology can bring the power of the experimental method and invasive neuroscientific techniques to bear on the question, but it is limited to the study of laboratory animals.

    Because the two approaches complement one another, together they can provide evidence for points of view that neither can defend individually.

5. Two Examples of BS (Bad Science)

-   end today's lecture with two examples of bad science (BS)
-   you might think it odd to begin a course on biopsychology by considering two bad examples of its science; this is done for two reasons:

    1) because disciplines learn from their mistakes, understanding biopsychology's previous errors provides insights into what it is today; and

    2) and it will make you a better consumer of scientific research--it will help you develop a healthy skepticism

a. Taming a Charging Bull with Caudate Stimulation

-    the biopsychology Jose Delgado implanted an electrode into the caudate nucleus of a bull
-   each time the bull charged, Delgado delivered a stimulation to its caudate nucleusthrough the implanted electrode by activating a hand-held radio transmitter
-   this stopped the charge; after a few attempts the bull stood tamely as Delgado strode about the ring
-   Delgado and the popular press declared this a major discovery, the discovery of the caudate taming center. It was even suggested that caudate stimulation might cure human psychopaths.

b. Prefrontal Lobotomy *(use Digital Image Archive, Chpt 1, CH01F08.BMP - CH01F10.BMP)*

-   in 1949, Dr. Egas Moniz was awarded a Nobel prize for developing a treatment for mental illness: prefrontal lobotomy, a form of neurosurgery that cuts the connections between the prefrontal lobes and the rest of the brain
-   Moniz based his technique on a report that a chimpanzee (Becky) was easier to handle after part of her prefrontal lobes had been destroyed in an experiment
-   following the initial reports by Moniz of the operation's beneficial effects, it was performed on mentally ill patients all over the world (over 40,000 in the U.S.A. alone)
-   various forms of the operation were devised such as the transorbital lobotomy procedure, which was performed by inserting an icepick-like device through the eye sockets, often in the doctor's office

6. **Class Discussion**

    -   guide the discussion to the following points and issues

    a. **What was wrong with Delgado's claims?**

        -   there are many ways that stimulation might stop a charging bull other than by taming it (e.g., the stimulation might have been painful, blinded the bull, made it sick, or made movement difficult)
        -   when there is more than one reasonable interpretation of a behavior, the general rule is to favor the most simple one; this rule is called *__Morgan's Canon__*
        -   in fact, analyses of the filmed record of this event strongly supports a more simple interpretation: the left and right caudate are motor structures and stimulating one often causes an animal to walk in circles. This appears to be what happened here; the bull was left confused and incapable of charging, but not tamed.
        -   Why do you think that an experienced scientist like Delgado would stage events like this for the popular press and exaggerate their significance?
        -   Why do you think the popular press and general public were so gullible?

    b. **What was wrong with Moniz's claims?**

        -   the surgery was based on the study of only one subject (Becky), and a nonhuman at that
        -   it is difficult to see how one could conclude that an operation that would eliminate the adaptive defensive reactions of a chimpanzee to an experimenter would help the mentally ill
        -   Moniz and the others who prescribed prefrontal lobotomy were not in a position to be objective in its evaluation, nor were they trained to perform such evaluation studies. Early reports of the benefits of prefrontal lobotomy were based on poorly controlled studies that focused on <u>manageability</u> and were published by Moniz himself.
        -   after many thousands of people had been lobotomized, controlled studies by objective researchers revealed terrible side effects, e.g., "vegetable-like behavior", urinary <u>incontinence</u>, epilepsy, loss of moral judgment (such as masturbating in public)
        -   Moniz was a physician, not a researcher; what were the repercussions of this?
        -   To what extent do you think that Moniz's claims were widely accepted by other physicians because they had no research training?
        -   To what extent do you think that Moniz's claims were widely accepted because there were no effective ways of treating mental illness at the time?
        -   Could such a travesty happen today?

Suggested Web Resources for Lecture 1b:

Moniz and The Prefrontal Lobotomy: *http://www.pbs.org/wgbh/aso/databank/entries/dh35lo.html*

> From WGBH Boston and the Public Broadcasting Service (PBS), a page about Moniz and the prefrontal lobotomy.

A History of Psychosurgery: *http://www.epub.org.br/cm/n02/historia/psicocirg_i.htm*

> From the Brain and Mind website at the State University of Campinas in Brazil, an easy-to-read history of psychosurgery. See also:

> > *http://neurosurgery.mgh.harvard.edu/psysurg.htm*

> A text-only site about psychosurgery, both historically and in the modern-day; moderately difficult but very informative.

Lecture 2a

EVOLUTION AND GENETICS

Outline

1. The Theory of Evolution

2. Behavior and Evolution
   a. Social dominance
   b. Courtship displays

3. Human Evolution

4. Fundamental Genetics

5. Human Genome Project

Lecture Notes

1. The Theory of Evolution

- *On the Origins of the Species* (Darwin, 1859)
- Darwin's theory that species undergo gradual orderly change is the most influential in the biological sciences
- Darwin was not the first to propose this idea, but he was the first to provide strong evidence for it: (1) evidence from fossil records, (2) structural similarities among existing species, (3) programs of selective breeding
- even stronger evidence comes from modern genetic studies and from observations of evolution in progress; e.g., Grant's (1991) study of changes in Galápagos finches after a 1-year drought--beak size increased in response to shortage of small seeds
- Darwin was also the first to suggest the mechanism by which evolution takes place: **natural selection**
- the evidence for the theory of evolution is unassailable; it meets with no significant opposition from the biological community

2. Evolution and Behavior

- early studies of evolution focused on structure; behavior also plays an important role in determining an organism's **fitness** (ability to pass on genes to future generations)
- the contributions of some behaviors (e.g., eating, sexual behavior, predatory behavior) are obvious; others are less obvious but no less important; two examples are social aggression and courtship displays

a. Social Dominance
   - the males of many species establish hierarchies of social dominance by combative encounters with other males of the species
   - social dominance influences evolution because dominant males (or females, in some species) are able to copulate more. For example, in a study of 10 bull elephant seals McCann (1981) found that the highest ranking bull accounted for 37% of copulations; the lowest ranking bull accounted for only 1%.

b. Courtship Displays
   - courtship displays precede copulation in many species
   - copulation is unlikely to occur if one partner fails to respond appropriately to displays of the other
   - courtship displays have an important function in evolution because they promote the formation of new species

- an idiosyncratic courtship display can form a **reproductive barrier** that is as effective as geographic separation

3. Human Evolution

- 600 million years ago the first single cell organisms lived in the oceans
- 450 million years ago, the first **chordates** evolved
- 425 million years ago, the first chordates with backbones (i.e., **vertebrates**) evolved; they were bony fishes
- 410 million years ago, the first bony fishes ventured onto land to escape stagnant pools and take advantage of untapped food sources; the Florida walking catfish is a survivor of this stage
- 400 million years ago, the first amphibians evolved; they are born in water and spend their larval stage there, but as adults they have legs and lungs and can survive on land
- 300 million years ago the first **reptiles** evolved from amphibians; they spend the first stage of their lives in the watery environment of a shell-covered egg; dry scales reduce water loss and allow adults to live away from water.
- 180 million years ago, during the age of dinosaurs, a line of reptiles evolved that fed their young through **mammary glands**; eventually, **mammals** stopped laying eggs and nurtured their young in the watery environment of their bodies
- today, there are 14 different orders of mammals; the one we belong to is <u>primates</u>; there are five different groups of primates: **prosimians, old-world monkeys, new-world monkeys, apes,** and **hominids**
- the order hominids is composed of two genera: <u>Homo</u> and <u>Australopithecus</u>
- 6 million years ago, Australopithecus is thought to have evolved from a species of African apes
- Australopithecines were 1.3 meters (4 feet) tall, they had small brains, they had an upright walk, and they became extinct about 1 million years ago
- 1.5 million years ago the first Homo species (**Homo erectus**) is thought to have evolved from Australopithecus; Homo erectus used tools and fire, but had a small brain cavity
- 200,000 years ago, Homo erectus hominids were gradually replaced by **homo sapiens**
- 25,000 years ago, Neanderthals were replaced by **Cro-Magnons**

An Interesting Point: Though human attributes like big brain, upright posture, and free hands evolved hundreds of thousands of years ago, most uniquely human accomplishments occurred only within the last 25,000 years.

Thinking About Human Evolution:

When thinking about human evolution, keep the following 7 points in mind:
1) Evolution does not proceed in a straight line.
2) Homo sapiens do NOT represent evolutionary supremacy.
3) Evolution is not always a slow, gradual process.
4) Present species represent a fraction of the species that have evolved on earth.
5) Evolution is not a perfectionist.
6) Evolution is not always adaptive.
7) Similarities between species does not mean a common evolutionary origin: keep in mind the differences between *homologous structures* (with a common evolutionary origin) and *analogous structures* (with different but <u>convergent</u> evolutionary processes in their origins)

Evolution of the Human Brain *(see Digital Image Archive, Chpt 2., CH02F12.BMP)*

- size is not the key; there is no relationship between size and intellectual capacity in humans, and human beings do not have the largest brains in the animal kingdom.

- 3 key points about the evolution of the human brain:
  1) it has **increased in size** during the course of evolution.
  2) most of this increase in size has occurred in the **cerebrum.**
  3) increase in size of cerebrum has been accompanied by increased **convolutions** of the cortex.

BUT...more significant than the differences between the brains of different species is the similarities between them...all brains are composed of neurons, these neurons generally function in a similar fashion, and in most cases similar structures can be found between species.

4. Mendelian Genetics *(see Digital Image Archive, Chpt 2., CH02F13.BMP)*

- the key to Mendel's success is that he studied **dichotomous traits** (brown or white peas) and **true-breeding lines** (in which interbred members always produce offspring with the same trait(.
- **KEY FINDING:** although the offspring of first crosses ALL had brown seeds, 25% of the offspring of second crosses had white seeds; this disproved the then dominant view that offspring inherit their parents' characteristics
- Mendel proposed each dichotomous trait was due to two kinds of inherited factors: these are called **genes.** Furthermore, each individual contains two genes for each dichotomous trait; these are called **alleles.**
- these results led to Mendel's development of the concepts of:

  1) **dominant** and **recessive** traits (dominant traits appear in 100% of first crosses; recessive traits in about 25% of second crosses)
  2) **genotype** (genetic traits that can be passed on to offspring) and **phenotype** (the observable genetic traits of an organism)
  3) **homozygous** organisms (that possess identical genes for a trait) and **heterozygous** organisms (that possess different genes for a trait)

- in early 1900's genes were located on the paired thread-like structures in the nucleus of cells; these were called **chromosomes**; the strongest early evidence of this came from studies of **lnkage** between various traits in a species (such that individuals expressing one trait usually expressed several other *linked traits*). In each species, the number of clusters of linked traits equals the number of pairs of chromosomes, suggesting that the traits were *linked* by their presence on the same chromosome.
- **crossing over** *(see Digital Image Archive, Chpt 2., CH02F16.BMP)* explains why traits on a chromosome are not always linked (i.e., inherited together); crossing over is important because it allows increases species diversity.

5. Human Genome Project

- perhaps the most ambitious scientific project of all time; plan to map the location of each of the 200,000 genes located on the 46 chromosomes that human beings possess.

- once mapping is complete, the knowledge will be used to better understand and treat genetically-based diseases (e.g., by substituting healthy genes for flawed ones) and to better understand the genetic bases of behavior.

Suggested Web Sites for Lecture 2a

Charles Darwin: *http://www.brunette.brucity.be/PEGASE/darwin/endarwin.htm*

From BRUNETTE, an extensive biography of Charles Darwin and the development of his theory of evolution.

Evolution and the Brain: *http://www.neurophys.wisc.edu/braintest/index.htmlx*

From the University of Wisconsin, an site on the evolution of the brain, complete with downloadable images from brains across the phylogenetic tree.

The Human Genome Project: *http://www.ornl.gov/TechResources/Human_Genome/home.html*

Website of the Human Genome project, sponsored by the US Dept of Energy.

Tutorial on Mendelian Genetics: *http://www.biology.arizona.edu/mendelian_genetics/mendelian_genetics.html*

From The Biology Project at the University of Arizona; provides overviews and tutorials illustrating the basic principles of Mendelian genetics.

Lecture 2b

THINKING ABOUT THE
BIOLOGY OF BEHAVIOR

Outline

1. Thinking in Dichotomies

2. Current Thinking About the Biology of Behavior

    a. Physiological or Psychological?
    b. Inherited or Learned?
    c. A Summary Model

3. Putting Interactionist Thinking to the Test

Lecture Notes

1. **Thinking in Dichotomies**

    -   we tend to think about behavior in terms of mutually exclusive dichotomies
    -   this is revealed by two questions that students commonly ask:
        (1) Is it physiological or is it psychological?   *(2) Is it inherited or is it learned?*
    -   learning to ask the right questions is the first step to getting the right answers

2. **Current Thinking About the Biology of Behavior**

    a. Is Behavior Physiological or Psychological?

        -   this idea grew out of the conflict between science and the Roman church: **Cartesian dualism**
        -   many people believe that there is a purely psychological category of human existence (one that transcends physiology), but there is no evidence for this. Two lines of evidence bear on this question:
            1) brain manipulations can alter even the most complex psychological processes (e.g., memory, emotion, self-awareness;
            2) nonhuman organisms possess abilities that many people once believed to be psychological and thus purely human (e.g., Gallup's studies of self-awareness in chimpanzees)
        -   today, most scientists believe that physiological activity is the basis of psychological processes

    b. Is Behavior Inherited or Learned?

        -   the nature-nurture issue is an ancient one
        -   in this century, reflected in conflict between Watsonian **behaviorists** and European **ethologists**
        -   the discovery that factors other than genes and learning influence development (e.g., diet, stress, fetal environment) led to a reframing of the question; from "genes or learning?" to "genes or experience?"
        -   next it was argued that behavior always develops under the combined control of genes and experience, not one or the other; thus, the question became "How much is genetic, and how much is experience?"
        -   with regard to human behavior and genetics the sum is not equal to the parts
        -   all behavioral development depends totally on genetics and totally on experience; modern biopsychologists study how they interact

c. A 6-Part Model of the Biology of Behavior *(see Digital Image Archive, Chpt 2., CH02F03.BMP)*

- using this figure, note the convoluted interaction between evolution, genes, and experience in the way an organism behaves in a given situation. Note that behavior influences and organism's experience as well as its evolutionary success.

3. Thinking Interactively About Behavioral Development

- thinking in terms of dichotomies is so pervasive that it is sometimes hard to think about the effects of genetics and experience on behavioral development interactively. To help you, here are three examples:

1) **Phenylketonuria** (PKU):

- is a form of mental retardation; it results from the accumulation of **phenylalanine** in the body; sufferers lack the gene for **phenylalanine hydroxylase**, which converts phenylalanine to tyrosine; they develop the disorder only if they consume phenylalanine-rich foods during development; it is diagnosed by high levels of **phenylpryruvic acid** in the urine; it is treated by keeping sufferers on a phenylalanine-free diet during childhood.

2) **Genetics and Learning:**

- Tryon raised **maze-bright** and **maze-dull** strains of rats; however, the maze-bright rats do better than the maze-dull only if they are both raised in impoverished environments (if they are both raised in enriched environments, the differences disappear); maze-bright rats are not generally more intelligent, they do better because they are less emotional.

3) **Development of Bird Song:** *(see Digital Image Archive, Chpt 2., CH02F24.BMP)*

- Some birds learn to sing by hearing conspecific songs early in life. Research in white-crowned sparrows has revealed an interesting gene-experience interaction: white-crown sparrows more readily learn the songs of their own species, and, they learn them more readily early in life. Zebra finches and white-crowned sparrows are **age-limited learners**, meaning that once the bird has developed an adult song it crystallizes, remaining unchanged for life. In contrast, male canaries are **open-ended learners**, meaning that they can add new songs to their repertoire each mating season.

4) Twin Studies:

- studies such as the **Minnesota Study** have found high correlations between the I.Q.s of identical twins separated at birth; **heritability estimates** based on these studies average about .70.

Q: *What does this mean? Is I.Q. 70% genetic?*

A: *Heritability estimates estimate the proportion of variability in a particular trait that results from genetic variation...that is, the contribution of genetic differences to phenotypic differences between individuals. They do NOT estimate the relative contribution of genes versus environment to development.*

- there are no psychological differences that do not have a genetic component; it is important to keep in mind that genetics alter the development of behavior by influencing an organism's experience of its surroundings, causing individuals with similar genetic endowment to seek out similar environments and experiences.

Conclusion:

- behavior is not a consequence of physiology or psychology, or of nature or nurture...it is the product of neural activity shaped by interactions among genes, which are the products of evolution, experience, and an organism's present situation.

Suggested Websites for Lecture 2b

Development of Bird Song: *http://instruct1.cit.cornell.edu/Courses/bionb420.07/klidoshore/zebrafinchsong.wav*

A fabulous site describing the anatomy, physiology and development of bird song in the zebra finch…check out the audio sample of its song!

Genetics and Learning: *http://piebald.princeton.edu/mb427/1997/students/learning/main.html*

Nice collection of links related to genetics and learning and memory in a variety of species, including mice, Aplysia, and human beings.

Twin Studies: *http://www.twinspace.com/outlinestudy.html*

A site devoted to twin studies into the role of genetics in trait development; in particular, see the link to Monozygotic Twins Reared Apart, a look at two subjects from the Minnesota Twins Reared Apart study.

---

*Thinking clearly about the biology of behavior is as important
in every-day life as it is in the biopsychology laboratory.*

Lecture 3a

**THE GROSS ANATOMY
OF THE NERVOUS SYSTEM**

Outline

1. Divisions of the Nervous System

2. Orientation and Direction in the Vertebrate Nervous System

3. The Meninges and Ventricles

4. The Five Major Divisions of the Brain

     a. Myelencephalon
     b. Metencephalon
     c. Mesencephalon
     d. Diencephalon
     e. Telencephalon

5. Summary of the Human Brain

Lecture Notes

1. Divisions of the Nervous System *(use Digital Image Archive, Figure CH03F02.BMP)*

- the nervous system can be divided into **2 divisions** along several different criteria

    A) **CNS** vs. **PNS** *(use Digital Image Archive, Figure CH03F03.BMP)*; defined by the CNS being within the bony skull and verterbral column;

    B) **brain** vs. **spinal cord**: comprise the CNS.

    C) **somatic** vs. **autonomic**: comprise the PNS.

    D) **efferent** vs. **afferent**: refers to whether nerves bring sensory information into the CNS *(afferent)* or carry motor commands away from the CNS *(efferent)*.

    E) **sympathetic** vs. **parasympathetic:** the two branches of the autonomic branch of the PNS.

- the **cranial nerves** are a special group of nerves that leave the CNS from the brain, through the skull, rather than from the spinal cord.

2. Orientation and Direction in the Vertebrate Nervous System *(use Digital Image Archive, Figure CH03F18.BMP)*

- First axis: **anterior** means toward the nose or front; **posterior** means toward the tail or back
- Second axis: **dorsal** is toward the surface of the back or top of the head (as in dorsal fin); **ventral** indicates the surface of the chest or bottom of the head
- Third axis: **medial** is toward the midline of the body; **lateral** indicates outside or away from the midline

3. The Meninges and Ventricles *(use Digital Image Archive, Figure CH03F03.BMP)*

- the CNS is hollow; the **central canal** in the spinal cord and the **ventricles** in the brain provide nourishment and remove waste from the brain
- there are four cerebral ventricles: the two **lateral ventricles**, the **third ventricle**, and the **fourth ventricle**
- the brain is wrapped in three membranes (the **meninges**) *(use Digital Image Archive, Figure CH03F04.BMP)*: (1) the **dura mater** (*tough mother;* outside), (2) the **arachnoid mater** (*spidery mother;* middle) and (3) the **pia mater** (*gentle mother;* inside)
- **cerebrospinal fluid** is manufactured by **choroid plexuses**, which are capillary networks that protrude into the ventricles from the arachnoid **menynx**; it circulates through ventricular system and the **subarachnoid space**, and it is absorbed into large channels called **sinuses** in the dura mater and then into the blood stream

4. **The Five Major Divisions of the Brain** (a brain model is useful for teaching this section)

- I am going to describe the five divisions of the mammalian brain in ascending order; higher structures have less reflexive and more complex functions, and they are more recently evolved structures
- the nervous system develops from a layer of epidermal cells in the embryo called the **neural plate**; the neural plate folds over on itself to form the **neural tube**
- the brain develops from three swellings at one end of the neural tube: (1) the **hind brain,** (2) the **midbrain (mesencephalon)**, and (3) the **forebrain** *(use Digital Image Archive, Figure CH03F21.BMP)*
- the hind brain develops into the **myelencephalon** and the **metencephalon**; the forebrain develops into the **diencephalon** and the **telencephalon** (also called the **cerebral hemispheres**)
- the term "**brain stem**" refers to the stem on which the cerebral hemispheres rest (myelencephalon + metencephalon + mesencephalon + diencephalon = brain stem)

- this figure illustrates the 5 major divisions of the brain *(use Digital Image Archive, Figure CH03F22.BMP)*; **we will now examine each of these divisions, beginning with the most posterior structure.**

a. Myelencephalon *(use Digital Image Archive, Figure CH03F23.BMP)*

- the myelencephalon is commonly called the **medulla**; it is composed of major ascending and descending tracts and a network of small nuclei in its core
- the core network of nuclei is the **reticular formation**; the reticular formation also composes the core of the hindbrain and midbrain; it is thought to be an arousal system, and is thus sometimes called the **reticular activating system** (reticulum means little net)

b. Metencephalon *(use Digital Image Archive, Figure CH03F23.BMP)*

- the metencephalon has two parts: the cerebellum (little brain) and pons (bridge)
- the cerebellum has a sensorimotor function; the pons is visible as a swelling on the inferior surface; it contains the reticular formation
- neural tracts ascend and descend through this area

c. Mesencephalon *(use Digital Image Archive, Figure CH03F24.BMP)*

- the mesencephalon is composed of the tectum and tegmentum
- the tectum is composed of the superior colliculi and the inferior colliculi; the tegmentum contains the reticular formation, the red nucleus (sensorimotor), the substantia nigra (sensorimotor); and the periaqueductal gray (mediates analgesia)

d. Diencephalon *(use Digital Image Archive, Figure CH03F25.BMP)*

- the **thalamus** and **hypothalamus** are the two main structures of the diencephalon
- the thalamus is the top of the brain stem; some thalamic nuclei are **sensory relay nuclei**; (e.g., **lateral geniculate nuclei**, vision; **medial geniculate nuclei**, audition; **ventral posterior nuclei**, touch); the **massa intermedia** runs through the **third ventricle** connecting the two lobes of the thalamus
- the **hypothalamus** is just below the thalamus ("hypo" means below); the **pituitary gland** is suspended from the hypothalamus; lesioning and stimulating the hypothalamus influences motivated behavior
- the **mammillary bodies** are two small bumps visible on the inferior surface, just behind the hypothalamus
- **optic chiasm**; the X-shaped **decussation** of the **optic nerves** (second cranial nerves) are just in front of the pituitary

e. Telencephalon *(use Digital Image Archive, Figure CH03F27.BMP and CH03F28.BMP)*

- also called the cerebral hemispheres; characterized by the cortex (bark) with its many convolutions, which are referred to as **gyri** (like hills) or **fissures** (like valleys).
- the telencephalon is the largest division of human brain; large tracts called **commissures** connect the two hemispheres; the **corpus callosum** is the largest commissure
- this division mediates most complex functions
- the four lobes of the cerebral hemispheres *(use Digital Image Archive, Figure CH03F28.BMP)* are defined by the fissures of the cerebral cortex. The four lobes are:

    (1) **frontal lobe:** superior to the **lateral fissure**   and anterior to the **central fissure;**
    (2) **temporal lobe:** inferior to the lateral fissure
    3) **parietal lobe:** posterior to the central fissure
    (4) **occipital lobe:** posterior to the temporal lobe and the parietal lobe

- note the following additional structures of the neocortex: **longitudinal fissure** (between the hemispheres), precentral gyri (in frontal lobe; primary motor cortex), **postcentral gyri** (in parietal lobe; primary somatosensory cortex), **superior temporal gyri** (in the temporal lobe; auditory cortex), and **prefrontal cortex** (the nonmotor portion of frontal lobe)

5. **Summary of the Human Brain** *(use Digital Image Archive, Figure CH03F32.BMP)*

- review the structures described in this lecture from this figure of the human brain

Suggested Websites for Lecture 3a

Autonomic Nervous System: *http://www.ndrf.org/*

The National Dysautonomia Research Foundation site; good overview of function and dysfunction of the ANS, including disorders like Shy-Drager Syndrome, Guillain Barre Syndrome, and more well-known disorders like diabetes and Parkinson's Disease.

Neuro-mneumoics: *http://www.telusplanet.net/public/jwberger/mneumonx.html*

Old, new and skewed ways to remember your neuroanatomy!

Ventricles and Cerebrospinal Fluid: *http://weber.u.washington.edu/~chudler/vent.html*

From Dr. Eric Chudler's at the University of Washington; good review of ventricular anatomy, CSF production and flow, and links to related sites.

Interactive Brain Atlas: *http://www9.biostr.washington.edu/da.html*

From the Digital Anatomist project at the University of Washington; from this page select the Interactive Brain Atlas for a fabulous collection of images in many different planes of section, digital recreations of different functional systems in the nervous system, and a good section on cerebrovasculature. *Instructors: Check out the Neurosyllabus site; it includes images from the Interactive Brain Atlas, complemented with text, that are organized into functional chapters.*

Lecture 3b

NEURONS, GLIA and
THE GENERAL LAYOUT of THE NERVOUS SYSTEM

Outline

1. Neurons and Glia

    a. Neurons
    b. Glial Cells and Satellite Cells

2. Divisions of the Nervous System

Lecture Notes

1. Neurons and Glia

- the gross structures of the nervous system discussed previously are made up of hundreds of billions of different cells that are either **neurons** or **glia.**

a. Neurons

- most of you have seen a diagram of a neuron like this *(use Digital Image Archive, Figure CH03F05.BMP)*

- this is a schematic drawing of a multipolar motor neuron; don't be misled by its familiar shape, as neurons come in a wide variety of sizes and shapes. The following are its 9 parts:

    1) a semipermeable **cell membrane**. The cell membrane is semipermeable because of special proteins that allows chemicals to cross the membrane (*(use Digital Image Archive, Figure CH03F07.BMP)* **this semipermeability is critical to the normal** activity of the neuron. The inside of the cell is filled with **cytoplasm** (*(use Digital Image Archive, Figure CH03F06.BMP)*

    2) a **cell body** (soma) which is the metabolic center of the cell. The soma also contains the **nucleus** of the neuron, which contains cell's DNA *(use Digital Image Archive, Figure CH03F06.BMP)*

    3) **dendrites,** shorter processes emanating from the cell body that receive information from synaptic contacts with other neurons;

    4) a single **axon**, that projects away from the cell body; this process may be as long as a meter!

    5) **axon hillock,** the junction between cell body and axon; a critical structure in the conveyance of electrical signals by the neuron.

    6) multiple **myelin sheaths.** These are formed by **oligodendroglia** in CNS and **Schwann** cells in PNS; they insulate the axon and assist in its conduction of electrical signals.

    7) **nodes of Ranvier**, the small spaces between adjacent myelin sheaths;

    8) **buttons,** the branched endings of the axon that release chemicals that allow the neuron to communicate with other cells; and

    9) **synapses,** the points of communication between the neuron and other cells (neurons, muscle fibers).

- this particular cell is called a **multipolar neuron** (because it has multiple dendrites and an axon extending from soma). There are also **monopolar neurons, bipolar neurons,** and **interneurons** that have no axons at all *(use Digital Image Archive, Figure CH03F08.BMP)*

b. **Glial Cells and Satellite Cells**

- neurons are interspersed with other cells, which are called **glial cells** (neuroglia) in the CNS and **satellite cells** in the PNS

- these cells provide both physical and functional support to neurons

- the glial cells and satellite cells that form the myelin sheaths of axons in the CNS and PNS are **oligodendroglia** and **Schwann cells**, respectively *(use Digital Image Archive, Figure CH03F10.BMP)*. **Multiple sclerosis** results from damage to the these glial cells, which impairs the ability of axons to conduct information (in the form of electrical signals) through the nervous system.

- **astroglia** are the largest of the glial cells; they are found only in the CNS, where they support neurons, absorb debris, and participate in the **blood-brain barrier**

Suggested Websites for Lecture 3b:

Neurons and Glia: *http://weber.u.washington.edu/~chudler/introb.html*

    From Dr. Chudler at the University of Washington; from here select "Neurons" to find links to pages about neurons, glia, and a photo gallery of cells.

Neuroanatomy Quiz: *http://psychlab1.hanover.edu/Classes/Neuro/*

    A quick quiz on neuroanatomy; part of Dr John Krantz's study aids and tutorials for biopsychology.

Lecture 3c

NEUROANATOMICAL METHODS

Outline

1. Picking the Correct Level of Analysis

2. Selectivity of Neural Stains

3. The Golgi Stain

4. The Nissl Stain

5. Myelin Stains

6. Electron Microscopy

7. Methods for Tracing Neural Pathways

    a. Anterograde Tracing
    b. Retrograde Tracing

Lecture Notes

1. Picking the Correct Level of Analysis

- have you ever heard the expression, "He can't see the forest for the trees?" It is an apt expression for anyone involved in biopsychological research, because it means that when something is studied in great detail, it is often difficult to identify obvious general principles.
- the opposite is also be true; if one takes a broad perspective in research key details can be missed
- in this course, you will learn about important discoveries made by biopsychologists taking general approaches (e.g., in the study of **lateral asymmetry**) and by those taking specific approaches (e.g., in the study of learning at individual synapses in *Aplysia*); the task of the biopsychologist is to select a level of analysis that is appropriate to the question at hand
- there a tendency to think that more detail is better, but this is not always true; total understanding can result only from the **convergence** of studies at all levels of detail
- today I am going to describe different methods of studying neuroanatomy that vary greatly in their ability to reveal detail

2. Selectivity of Neural Stains

- if you look at unstained CNS tissue under a powerful microscope, you see a morass of neuron cell bodies, neural processes, supporting glial cells, and blood vessels; from this jumble it is difficult to tell anything; in order to obtain a more informative view, the tissue must first be stained
- to be useful stains must be **selective**; they must stain some components of the tissue, but not others
- a stain that highlights everything is not useful; it just transforms an uncolored jumble into a colored jumble
- selective stains work because they color only the components of interest

3. The **Golgi Stain**

    - The Golgi stain was the first stain to be discovered (1870); it was accidentally formulated when **Camillo Golgi** was trying to develop a **meninges** stain; he mixed **potassium dichromate** and **silver nitrate** and the resulting **silver chromate** stained neurons entirely black
    - the amazing thing about the Golgi stain is that, for some unknown reason, it stains only a few neurons on each slide; if all the neurons were stained, nothing would be visible
    - the Golgi stain permitted individual neurons to be observed for the first time; they were visible in silhouette only (no cellular details) as axons, dendrites, and the soma were stained completely black; only rarely is an entire neuron visible in one thin slice
    - the first view of **synapses** was obtained when, by chance, two adjacent neurons were stained

4. The **Nissl Stain**

    - the **Nissl stain** was developed by **Franz Nissl** in 1880; this stain does not affect axons and dendrites but has a strong affinity for structures in the **cell body**, which were initially called **Nissl bodies** now we know that Nissl bodies are **ribosomes**, the structures in cell bodies that manufacture proteins under the direction of **mRNA**; all cells have ribosomes, but neuron cell bodies have more and thus stain much more darkly
    - the Nissl stain permitted the first view of structures inside a neuron; the Nissl stain is useful for counting the cell bodies in an area
    - cresyl violet is the most common Nissl stain

5. **Myelin Stains**

    - first method for studying axons
    - shows **myelinated** areas of nervous system, but proved a poor method for studying specific pathways because: 1) didn't work on unmyelinated paths; 2) could not show where axons began or ended, as initial segment of axon and its terminal branches are not myelinated; and 3) these stains did not allow one axon to be discriminated from another.

6. Methods for **Tracing Neural Pathways**:

    -   in order to understand how the nervous system works, the pathways that connect various structures to one another must be identified (bundles of axons in the CNS are called **tracts** and those in the PNS are called **nerves**)
    -   tracing neural pathways is difficult because each neuron receives inputs from many neurons and in turn projects to many neurons
    -   there are two kinds of tracing:

    a. **Anterograde Tracing** (indicates where the axons leaving a particular area go)

        - used when you want to know where a neurons axons project to
        - typically involves the injection of a **tritiated** amino acid into the region of the neural cell body (tritiated means that the hydrogen atoms in the amino acid have been replaced by **tritium**, the radioactive isotope of hydrogen)
        - **amino acids** are the building blocks of all **proteins**, which are the main constituents of neurons
        - the **cell body** is the metabolic center of the neuron; in the cell body, the tritiated amino acids are taken and are incorporated into proteins, which are then transported throughout the neuron including down its axon to its terminal regions.
        - after a few days, the brain is removed and sliced and subjected to **autoradiography** (see text, p. 122); the slices are coated with a photographic emulsion and put in the dark for a few days
        - then the slices are developed like a film, and dark spots indicate the location of radioactivity concentrated in the axon terminals of those neurons with cell bodies in the area of the injection

    b. Retrograde Tracing (indicates where the axons entering a particular area come from)

- used when you want to trace the path from the axon from its terminal fields back to the cell body
- chemicals that are readily taken up by the terminal buttons are injected into the axonal area and over the course of a few days are transported backward along the axon to the soma
- the brain is then removed and sliced; slices are treated to reveal the location of chemicals

7. **Electron Microscopy**

- when viewing slides under a **light microscope**, the magnification limit without substantial distortion is 1,500 times due to the nature of light
- greater magnification can be obtained by using an **electron microscope** (because **electrons** are smaller than particles of light)
- very thin brain slices are coated with an electron-absorbing substance; different parts of neurons take up the substance to different degrees; then a beam of electrons is passed through the slide onto a photographic film to produce an **electron micrograph**
- the electron micrograph reveals minute cellular details
- **scanning electron microscopy** can render 3-D images of neural structures

Conclusion:

- neuroanatomy is a field built on **converging operations**; each technique provides only a limited view of the brain, but much has been learned about brain structure by considering together the results of various kinds of staining procedures

Suggested Websites for Lecture 3a:

Neurohistology: *http://education.vetmed.vt.edu/Education/Curriculum/VM8054/Labs/Lab9/Lab9.htm*

    From Dr. Thomas Caceci at the Virginia/Maryland Regional College of Veterinary Medicine, an excellent neurohistology resource; some description of the techniques, and lots of nice figures covering all levels of the neuraxis.

Camillo Golgi:

http://www.nobel.se/laureates/medicine-1906-1-bio.html and *http://www.nobel.se/essays/golgi/index.html*

    These provide a biography and a review of the life's work of Camillo Golgi.

        See also: *http://www.cajal.csic.es/valverde/golgi1.htm*

    From the Instituto Cajal in Madrid, Spain; a site devoted to images of neural tissue prepared with the Golgi technique.

Microscopic Techniques and Images: *http://www.pbrc.hawaii.edu/~kunkel/*

    Dr. Dennis Kunkel's microscopy site; brief review of light and electron microscopy at the "About Microscopy" page; go to "Image Gallery: Medical Images 1-4" to see various images of neural tissue and the "Light Microscopy Gallery: Neurotransmitters" to see images of several types of neurotransmitters (beautiful!).

Lecture 4a

THE GENERATION OF ACTION POTENTIALS

Outline:

1. Measuring the Membrane Potential

2. Squid Giant Motor Neurons

3. Resting Membrane Potential

4. Four Factors Determine the Ionic Distribution that Underlies the Resting Potential

   a. Random Motion
   b. Electrostatic Pressure
   c. Differential Permeability of the Membrane
   d. Sodium-Potassium Pumps

5. Postsynaptic Potentials

6. Generation of Action Potentials

7. Ionic Events Underlying Action Potentials

Lecture Notes

1. Measuring the Membrane Potential *(use Digital Image Archive, CH04F02.BMP)*

   - our current understanding of how information is sent from the dendrites and soma of a neuron to its terminals has come from the study of their **membrane potential** (the difference in electrical charge between the inside and the outside of the neuron).
   - to record a membrane potential two electrodes are needed: an **intracellular** electrode and an **extracellular** electrode
   - intracellular electrodes must be **microelectrodes**; they are usually made from **saline-filled micropipettes** by heating and pulling apart a fine glass tube with an **electrode puller**

2. Squid Giant Motor Neurons

   - most of what we know about the resting potential and other aspects of neural function was originally revealed by studying the **squid giant motor neuron**; its axon is 0.5 mm in diameter, almost 35 times larger than the 0.015 mm in mammalian motor neurons.
   - motor neurons are multipolar neurons that terminate on a muscle
   - remember these are squid "giant motor neurons", not "giant squid" motor neurons (one confused student asked if giant squids ever attacked submarines *8}
   - fortunately, most discoveries about the basic electrical activity of squid giant motor neurons holds for other multipolar neurons

3. Resting Membrane Potential *(use Digital Image Archive, CH04F03.BMP)*

    - when both intracellular and extracellular electrodes are outside a neuron, the difference between the electrical potentials at their tips is zero; as the intracellular electrode penetrates the neuron, the potential jumps to about **-70 millivolts** (the inside is 70 millivolts less than the outside)
    - this is the **resting potential** of the neuron
    - the resting potential results from the fact that positively and negatively charged <u>ions</u> become distributed unequally on the two sides of the neural membrane: (1) the concentration of NA^+ is higher outside, (2) the concentration of Cl^- is higher outside, (3) the concentration of K^+ is higher inside, and (4) various negatively charged protein ions are trapped

4. Four Factors Affect the Ionic Distribution That Underlies the Resting Potential *(use Digital Image Archive, CH04F04.BMP)*

    -   four factors interact to produce the resting membrane potential; two **passive** (non-energy-consuming) factors act to distribute ions equally across the membrane (**homogenizing factors**), and one passive and one active factor act to distribute ions unequally across the membrane

    a. **Random Motion** (passive)
        - ions in solution are in random motion
        - thus, any time that there is an accumulation of a particular class of ions in one area, the probability is increased that random motion will drive ions out of this area (because there are more ions available to leave) and the probability is decreased that random motion will drive more ions into the area (because there are fewer ions available to come in)

    b. **Electrostatic Pressure** (passive)
        - like charges repel and opposite charges attract; therefore electrostatic pressure disperses any accumulation of positive or negative charges in an area

    c. **Differential Permeability of the Membrane** (passive)
        - ions pass through membrane at special pores called <u>ion channels</u>
        - when neurons are at rest, the membrane is: totally resistant to the passage of protein ions, extremely resistant to the passage of Na^+ ions, moderately resistant to the passage of K^+ ions, and only slightly resistant to the passage of Cl^- ions

    d. **Sodium-Potassium Pumps** (active)
        - active (energy-consuming) mechanisms in the neural membrane continuously transfer Na^+ ions out of the neuron and K^+ ions in

5. Postsynaptic Potentials

    - now that you understand the state of resting neurons, let's see how signals are created in them; first **postsynaptic potentials** are produced by the action of **neurotransmitters** released by **presynaptic neurons**; input across some synapses is excitatory, across others it is inhibitory
    - **excitatory postsynaptic potentials** (EPSPs) are **depolarizations**; they increase the likelihood that a neuron will fire
    - **inhibitory postsynaptic potentials** (IPSPs) are **hyperpolarizations**; they decrease the likelihood that a neuron will fire
    - postsynaptic potentials have three important properties: (1) they are **graded** (their amplitude is proportional to the intensity of the input; that is, stronger stimuli produce bigger EPSPs and IPSPs); (2) they are **transmitted decrementally** (as they passively spread from their site of generation, they get weaker as they go, like sound through air); and (3) they are **transmitted rapidly** (like electricity through a cable, so rapidly that transmission is usually regarded as being instantaneous)

6. Generation of Action Potentials

    - **action potentials** (APs; neuron firing) are triggered at the **axon hillock** when a neuron is depolarized to the point that the membrane potential at the axon hillock reaches about **-65 mV**; this is the **threshold of excitation** for many neurons
    - unlike EPSPs and IPSPs, APs are **not graded**; they are **all-or-none** (they occur full blown or not at all)
    - most neurons receive hundreds of synaptic contacts; what happens at any one synapse has very little effect on the firing of the neuron; whether or not a neuron fires is determined by the adding together (integration) of what goes on at many neurons
    - there are two kinds of neural integration:

        (1) spatial summation *(use Digital Image Archive, CH04F06.BMP)* which can involve EPSPs + EPSPs; IPSPs + IPSPs; or EPSPs + IPSPs; and

        (2) temporal summation *(use Digital Image Archive, CH04F07.BMP)* which can involve EPSPs + EPSPs or IPSPs + IPSPs. NOTE THAT EPSPs AND IPSPs CANNOT TEMPORALLY SUMMATE...due to the fact that just a single synapse is involved.

    - in a functioning neuron, both spatial and temporal summation go on continuously; synapses closer to the axon hillock have a larger effect on firing due to the decremental transmission of postsynaptic potentials

7. Ionic Events Underlying Action Potentials *(use Digital Image Archive, CH04F08.BMP)*

    - when the threshold of excitation (about -65mV) is reached, **voltage-gated Na$^+$ channels** open momentarily, and Na$^+$ ions rush into the neuron under tremendous pressure from both their concentration gradient and the electrostatic gradient; this drives the membrane potential to about +50 millivolts
    - at the same time, **voltage-gated K$^+$ channels** slowly begin to open. Most of these channels open at about the time that the membrane potential is about +50 mV. At this point, K$^+$ ions are driven out by the +50 millivolt charge and by their high internal concentration; this repolarizes the neuron and leaves it slightly **hyperpolarized** for a few milliseconds.
    - because only a few ions adjacent to the membrane are involved in the generation of an action potential, the resting potential is readily reestablished by the random motion of ions (AND NOT THE NA+/K+ PUMP!)

Summary

    - today we have seen how action potentials are generated; next lecture we will see how action potentials travel along an axon and trigger the release of neurotransmitter molecules from its buttons; we will also see how neurotransmitter molecules travel across the synapse and elicit postsynaptic potentials; thus returning us to the starting point of today's lecture and completing the cycle of neural conduction and synaptic transmission

Suggest Websites for Lecture 4a:

> **The Action Potential:** *http://weber.u.washington.edu/~chudler/ap.html*
>
> > From Dr. Chudler's excellent site at the University of Washington, a description of the action potential complete with the an animation and the "sounds" of an action potential.
>
> **Action Potential Animations:** *http://psych.hanover.edu/Krantz/neural/actionpotential.html*
>
> > From Dr. John Krantz at Hanover College, an animation of the physical factors involved in the action potential. A good introduction to ions, diffusion, complete with quizes.

Lecture 4b

AXONAL CONDUCTION AND
SYNAPTIC TRANSMISSION

Outline:

1. Review

2. Conduction of Action Potentials

3. Refractory Periods

4. Synaptic Contacts and Transmission

    a. Diversity of Synaptic Contacts
    b. Synaptic Transmission

5. Neurotransmitters and Receptors

    a. Amino Acid Neurotransmitters
    b. Monoamine Neurotransmitters
    c. Acetylcholine
    d. Soluble Gas Neurotransmitters
    e. Neuropeptide Neurotransmitters

Lecture Notes

1. **Review**

    - you have already learned that neurotransmitters induce **EPSPs** and **IPSPs** on the postsynaptic membranes of the **dendrites** and **cell body**; that these **graded** potentials are transmitted **instantly** and **decrementally** to the **axon hillock**; that these EPSPs and IPSPs are **integrated** (summated); and that if the sum of the EPSPs and IPSPs at the hillock is a **depolarization** great enough to bring the membrane potential to its **threshold of excitation**, an **all-or-none action potential** is generated
    - today, you will learn how action potentials travel along the axon and how signals produced by them are transmitted across synapses

2. **Conduction of Action Potentials**

    - once an AP is generated at the axon hillock, it is transmitted along the axon; the purpose of axons is to transmit APs from the soma to the terminal buttons of the neuron
    - transmission of all-or-none APs along an axon is not like the transmission of graded postsynaptic potentials; transmission of EPSPs and IPSPs is <u>passive</u> (like electricity through a cable), thus it is instantaneous and decremental; whereas transmission of an AP along an axon is <u>active</u>, thus it is slower and nondecremental
    - to understand axonal transmission, think of the axon as a row of <u>voltage-gated</u> sodium channels
    - when voltage-gated sodium channels on the hillock membrane open, Na^+ ions rush in and a full blown AP is generated; the electrical disturbance thus created is transmitted passively to the next sodium channels along the axon, and like trap doors they open and another full-blown potential is generated there--and so on
    - in reality, the sodium channels are so tightly packed that it is best to think of APs as waves of depolarization spreading down an axon

- because the conduction of APs is an active process, there are two key differences between the conduction of APs and the conduction of PSPs:

(1) AP conduction is **slower**; and
(2) AP conduction is **nondecremental**; that is,
APs arriving at the end of the axon are just as large as those generated at the hillock

- APs also spread from the hillock back through the cell body and dendrites, but because the ion channels in the cell body and dendrites are **chemical-gated** rather than voltage-gated, transmission of action potentials through cell bodies and dendrites is passive
- many of the neurons in the CNS have no axons; they are **interneurons**; they have no action potentials; they are small, difficult to study, and not well understood; for example, in the human visual system, incoming signals are transmitted through four layers of neurons before reaching one with an axon
- transmission in the normal direction (**orthodromic stimulation**), from the hillock to the buttons, is called **anterograde transmission**; however, if the buttons are electrically stimulated, APs can be generated, and these are actively transmitted back to the hillock; this is called **retrograde transmission** (**antidromic stimulation**)
- I mentioned previously in the course that many axons are myelinated by **oligodendroglia** in the CNS and by **Schwann cells** in the PNS; myelination insulates the semipermeable axon membrane blocking the flow of ions through the axon at all but the **nodes of Ranvier**; paradoxically this actually improves transmission
- in myelinated axons, APs travel passively (decrementally and rapidly) between the nodes of Ranvier; but at each node there is a "pause" while a full-blown AP is generated
- this is called **saltatory conduction** ("saltatory" means to skip or jump); because much of the transmission of APs in myelinated axons is passive (from node to node), transmission in myelinated axons is faster and it requires less energy
- larger axons conduct faster; myelinated axons conduct faster: (1) large myelinated mammalian axons (e.g., axons of sensory and motor neurons; diameter = 0.015 mm) transmit at about 100 meters per second (about 224 miles per hour), (2) small unmyelinated mammalian axons conduct at about 1 meter per second (2.24 mph); and (3) squid giant motor axons (diameter = 0.5 mm), which are unmyelinated, conduct at 25 meters per second (56 mph)

3. Refractory Periods

- for a brief period of time (about 1 millisecond) after the onset of an action potential, another action potential cannot be elicited at the same point, no matter how intense the stimulation; this period is called the **absolute refractory period**
- a wave of "absolute refractoriness" spreads down the axon behind the action potential; a part of the membrane that has just participated in the transmission of an action potential cannot fire again until it has been repolarized; this keeps the spread of the action potential down the axon from reversing
- because the absolute refractory period is about 1 millisecond, neurons cannot normally fire more frequently than 1,000 times per second
- after the absolute refractory period, there is a period of time during which the neuron can fire again, but it takes a greater than normal level of stimulation to do it; this is called the **relative refractory period**; the relative refractory period is the reason why more intense stimulation produces more rapid firing

4. Synaptic Contacts and Transmission

a. Diversity of Synaptic Contacts

- in addition to axosomatic and axodendritic synapses there are: (1) **axoaxonic** synapses, (2) **dendrodendritic** synapses, (3) **dendroaxonic** synapses, (4) synapses between the main shafts of axons, (5) **nondirected synapses**
- some dendrodendritic synapses are **reciprocal** (they can transmit in either direction)
- many neurons have **autoreceptors** in their presynaptic membranes; these are stimulated by the neuron's own neurotransmitter and are thought to mediate negative feedback

- some synapses occur on little buds on dendrites; these buds are called **dendritic spines**; other dendritic synapses occur right on the dendrite shaft
- axoaxonic synapses mediate **presynaptic inhibition**; **postsynaptic inhibition** is mediated by axodendritic and axosomatic synapses
- most synapses that are discussed in textbooks are **directed synapses** (synapses where the site of release and the target site are in close apposition)
- there are also **nondirected synapses**; for example, some presynaptic axons have a **string-of-beads** appearance and the neurotransmitter is widely dispersed from each bead to many targets in the general area; this arrangement is common for monoamines
- in a sense, the **neuroendocrine system** has the most nondirected synapses; neurotransmitters (i.e., **neurohormones**) are released into the circulatory system by neurons and dispersed throughout the body

b. Synaptic Transmission *(use Digital Image Archive, Figure CH04F09.BMP)*

- much of what we know about synaptic transmission comes from the study of **neuromuscular junctions**; muscle cells are conveniently large and, unlike neurons, most muscle cells receive only one synapse; **acetylcholine** is the neurotransmitter at neuromuscular junctions
- the arrival of an AP at a terminal button opens **voltage-gated calcium channels** in the button membrane, and Ca^{++} ions enter the button
- the entry of the Ca^{++} ions causes the synaptic vesicles to fuse with the **presynaptic membrane** and empty their contents into the **synaptic cleft**--a process called **exocytosis**
- the released neurotransmitter substance moves to the **post-synaptic membrane**; there it binds to receptors for it in the postsynaptic membrane; there are specific receptors for each neurotransmitter
- as the synaptic vesicles combine with the presynaptic membrane during exocytosis, the button gets larger and larger, but bits of presynaptic membrane break off back into cytoplasm; in some cases the membrane bits are turned into vesicles and filled with neurotransmitter right in the button by a **cisterna**; in other cases, the bits are transported back to the cell body for recycling by the **Golgi apparatus** *(use Digital Image Archive, Figure CH03F06.BMP)*
- the binding of the neurotransmitter to its receptors can influence the postsynaptic neuron in one of two fundamentally different ways: *(use Digital Image Archive, Figure CH04F13.BMP)*

    (1) it can directly influence chemical-gated channels in the postsynaptic membrane and induce brief EPSPs or IPSPs; or (2) it can trigger chemical reactions in the cytoplasm of the postsynaptic neuron that lead to the production of chemicals, called **secondary messengers** (e.g., **cyclic AMP**), which can have more enduring and far-reaching effects on the sensitivity of the neuron

- neurotransmitters are **deactivated** in the synapse by one of two mechanisms: *(use Digital Image Archive, Figure CH04F14.BMP)*

    (1) first, it was found that acetylcholine is broken down by the enzyme **acetylcholinesterase,** and it was assumed that all neurotransmitters were deactivated by enzymes; (2) it now appears that all other neurotransmitters are deactivated by reuptake into the presynaptic neuron, where they are recycled

5. **Neurotransmitters and Receptors** *(use Digital Image Archive, Figure CH04F17.BMP)*

- neurotransmitters are of two types, **large-molecule neurotransmitters** and **small-molecule neurotransmitters**
- most small-molecule neurotransmitters have punctate, point-to-point effects; they are released in a pulse into synaptic clefts each time an action potential reaches a button
- they are synthesized in the cytoplasm of terminal buttons
- large-molecule neurotransmitters are released gradually in response to general increases in neuron firing; their effects are usually widespread because they are often released into extracellular fluid, the ventricles, or the bloodstream; they are thought to function as **neuromodulators**

- it was initially assumed that there is only one kind of receptor for each neurotransmitter; it is now clear that each neurotransmitter binds to more than one class of receptor; for example, **muscarinic** (found in internal organs) and **nicotinic** (found at neuromuscular junctions) acetylcholine receptors, with each subtype binding then producing fundamentally different responses
- receptor subtypes are located in different brain areas; this allows neurotransmitters to signal differently at various locations; postsynaptic neurons are differentially influenced based on the receptor subtype
- **ion-channel linked receptors** chemically open or close an ion channel inducing an immediate postsynaptic potential, these receptors are not prevalent but are fast acting
- **G-protein linked receptors** consist of a protein chain that winds in and out of the cell membrane seven times and each is located next to a guanine sensitive protein
- the binding breaks away the G-protein and leads to one of two actions; the subunit may move inside the surface of the membrane, binding to an ion channel to induce an EPSP or IPSP; the binding may trigger the synthesis of a second messenger that diffuses through the cytoplasm to bind to ion channels (for an EPSP or IPSP), influence the metabolic activities of the cell, or bind to DNA in the nucleus to influence gene expression
- G-protein linked receptors are more prevalent, are slower acting, longer lasting, and more diffuse than ion-channel linked receptors

a. *Amino Acid Neurotransmitters*
   - amino acids are the individual building blocks of proteins; they also serve as the transmitters at fast-acting, point-to-point synapses
   - there is conclusive evidence that **glutamate, aspartate, glycine**, and gamma-aminobutyric acid (**GABA**) are neurotransmitters
   - we get glutamate, aspartate, and glycine from the proteins that we eat; GABA is synthesized from glutamate, thus diet is important to "healthy" neurotransmission

b. *Monoamine Neurotransmitters*
   - monoamine neurotransmitters are formed by slight modification to amino acid molecules; thus the name "monoamine" (one amine)
   - they are often released from **string-of-beads** axons, and they have slow, lingering, diffuse effects; neurons that release monoamines typically have their cell bodies in the brain stem (e.g., the nigrostriatal dopamine pathway)
   - there are four monoamine neurotransmitters and they belong to one of two subclasses:
                     1) **catecholamines** or **indolamine**

     1) there are **three catecholamine** neurotransmitters: **dopamine, norepinephrine,** and **epinephrine**; all three are synthesized from the amino acid **tyrosine**; tyrosine is converted to L-DOPA, to dopamine, to norepinephrine, to epinephrine
     2) there is **one indolamine** neurotransmitter: **serotonin**; it is synthesized from the amino acid **tryptophan**

c. *Acetylcholine*
   - acetylcholine (ACH) is the small molecule transmitter at neuromuscular junctions, at many synapses in the ANS, and at some CNS synapses; it is created by addition of an **acetyl group** to a **choline** molecule; thus the name
   - acetylcholine is the only neurotransmitter known to be deactivated in the synapse by enzymatic degradation rather than by reuptake; it is deactivated by (**acetylcholinesterase**) (ACHE)

d. *Soluble Gas Neurotransmitters*
   - this class of recently identified neurotransmitters includes nitric oxide and carbon monoxide
   - the gasses are produced in the neural cytoplasm, diffuse immediately through the cell membrane into the extracellular fluid and into nearby cells to stimulate production of second messengers
   - they are difficult to study as they act rapidly and are immediately broken down, existing for only a few seconds

e. *Neuropeptide Transmitters*
- peptides are short chains of 10 or fewer amino acids; about 40 or 50 peptides are **putative neurotransmitters**; they are the largest neurotransmitters
- many peptides are released by endocrine glands into the bloodstream as well as by neurons; thus they have far-reaching diffuse effects
- peptides are synthesized by being cleaved from **polypeptide** chains containing between 10 and 100 amino acids; **proteins** are chains of over 100 amino acids
- neuropeptides are thought to function as <u>neuromodulators</u>; they are thought to adjust a neuron's sensitivity to fast-acting point-to-point neurotransmitters
- **coexistence** (neuropeptides are released from neurons that also release small-molecule neurotransmitters); it had been previously assumed that each neuron releases only one neurotransmitter

Summary *(use Digital Image Archive, Figure CH04F18.BMP)*.

- review the seven steps of synaptic transmission illustrated in this figure.

Suggested Websites for Lecture 4b:

Synaptic Transmission: *http://www.csuchico.edu/psy/BioPsych/neurotransmission.html*

From the Department of Psychology at Cal State, Chico, a nice page on synaptic transmission; includes some interesting neurotrivia and pointing quizes in several places.

Neurotransmitter Systems:

http://www.uams.edu/department_of_psychiatry/syllabus/NEUROTRA/Trans95.htm

From Dr. Jeremy Clothier at the University of Arkansas, good page on neurotransmitter systems. A bias toward the biogenic amines, perhaps...but some informative text and good figures of synthetic pathways and terminal distribution for each system under study. See also:

http://weber.u.washington.edu/~chudler/chnt1.html

More from the Dr. Eric Chudler at t he University of Washington, a good overview of synaptic transmission including synthesis, release, and degradation of neurotransmitters and neuropeptides

Lecture 5a

METHODS OF STUDYING THE NERVOUS SYSTEM

Outline

1. Methods of Visualizing the Living Human Brain
    a. Contrast X-rays
    b. Computerized Axial Tomography
    c. Magnetic Resonance Imaging
    d. Positron Emission Tomography
    e. Functional MRI

2. Recording Psychophysiological Signals
    a. Scalp Electroencephalography
    b. Measures of Somatic Nervous System Activity
    c. Autonomic Nervous System Activity

3. Invasive Physiological and Pharmacological Methods
    a. Stereotaxic Surgery
    b. Lesion Methods
    c. Electrical Stimulation
    d. Electrical Recording Methods
    e. Psychopharmacological Methods

4. Genetic Engineering
    a. Knockouts
    b. Gene replacement

Lecture Notes

1. **Methods of Visualizing the Living Human Brain**

    -   methods in this section explain how the nervous systems of living humans and animals can be studied

    a. **Contrast X-rays:**

    - to take an X-ray photograph of an object, a beam of X-rays is passed through it onto a photographic plate; any part of the object that absorbs X-rays differently than does the surrounding medium will be distinguishable
    - standard X-rays are of no use for studying the brain because the brain is composed of many overlapping structures that all absorb X-rays to about the same degree
    - the **contrast X-ray** is a method of solving this problem that can be used in some cases; a **radio-opaque material** is introduced into the structure of interest to make it "stand out" from the others on an X-ray photograph; for example, in **pneumoencephalography** air is worked into the ventricles after its injection into the spinal cerebrospinal fluid (it reveals enlarged or displaced ventricles), and in **angiography** radio-opaque dye is injected into the **carotid artery** (it reveals displacement or enlargement of blood vessels)

b. **Computerized Tomography** (CT)

- provides a 3-dimensional view of a structure; brain CT scans are usually composed of 8 or 9 horizontal sections
- the X-ray gun and the X-ray detector rotate in apposition around the brain at one level taking a series of measurements from which an image of one section is constructed; this is repeated at 8 or 9 different levels
- the CT-scan image of the brain is not sharp

c. **Magnetic Resonance Imaging** (MRI)

- it has higher powers of resolution than CT as X-rays aren't used
- the images are created from measurements of the waves emitted by **hydrogen atoms** when they are placed in a magnetic field; its clarity stems from the fact that neural structures differ considerably in their density of hydrogen atoms

d. **Positron Emission Tomography** (PET)
- PET is a method of highlighting brain areas that are active, rather than equally showing all brain structures
- the patient is injected with radio-active **2-deoxyglucose**; because 2-DG is structurally similar to glucose, it is taken up by neurons as if it were glucose; more active neurons need more energy and take up more 2-DG; unlike glucose, 2-DG cannot be metabolized by neurons and it accumulates in them
- the patient is injected with radio-active 2-DG and then engages in the activity under study (e.g., reading) while a **PET scan** of the brain is being taken; the PET scan reveals on a series of images of horizontal sections where radio-activity has accumulated, and thus it indicates what areas were particularly active during the test

e. **Functional MRI**
- allows brain activity to be measured via images of the increase in oxygen (blood) flow to the areas that are active
- its four advantages over PET include (1) nothing must be injected into the subject, (2) one image provides structural and functional ion formation, (3) the spatial resolution is better, and (4) changes can be measured in real time

2. **Recording Psychophysiological Signals**

a. Scalp Electroencephalography (EEG): *(use Digital Image Archive Figure CH05F07.BMP)*

- an EEG signal is the difference in the electrical potential between two large **scalp electrodes** as a function of time; in laboratory species, EEG activity is usually recorded through electrodes implanted in cortical or subcortical tissue
- EEG waves reflect the sum total of all of the electrical events in the head (APs, EPSPs, IPSPs, eye movements, blood flow, etc.); thus the EEG reveals little about the nature of the underlying neural activity
- its value lies in the fact that particular EEG wave forms are associated with particular states of consciousness; generally low-amplitude, fast EEG activity is associated with an alert aroused state; and high-amplitude, slow EEG activity (alpha waves) is associated with a relaxed but awake state
- EEG can be used to study brain activity in real time, in response to specific events. These are called **evoked potentials** *(use Digital Image Archive Figure CH05F09.BMP)*. Usually, many evoked potentials are used to generate an **averaged evoked potential** in order to reduce the noise of the background EEG activity *(use Digital Image Archive Figure CH05F10.BMP)*
- EEG recording is a valuable diagnostic tool; for example, the presence of high-amplitude spikes in the EEG (i.e., **epileptic spikes**) is the primary criterion for diagnosing epilepsy

b.   Measures of Somatic Nervous System Activity

1. **Electromyography** **(EMG)**
- an EMG signal is the changing difference in the voltage between two large electrodes placed on the skin above a large muscle; the amplitude of EMG signals indicates the combined level of tension in the underlying muscle
- the raw signals are usually **integrated**; the graph of the integrated activity is easier to interpret; the height of the curve of integrated EMG activity indicates the number of spikes in the EMG signal per unit of time *(use Digital Image Archive Figure CH05F11.BMP)*

2. **Electrooculography** **(EOG)**
- in EOG, eye movements are recorded by placing four electrodes around the eye; the signal results from the fact that the front of eye is more positively charged than the back
- direction of movement can be inferred from the relation between the activity recorded on two channels: (1) above vs. below and (2) left vs. right

c.   Autonomic Nervous System Activity

- **heart rate**; electrocardiogram (ECG)
- **blood pressure** is expressed as peak pressure during **systoles** over minimum pressure during **diastoles**; 130/70 mm/Hg is normal; greater than 150/90 is **hypertension**; the device commonly used to measure blood pressure is a **sphygmomanometer**
- plethysmography is the measurement of the volume of blood in a body structure (e.g., penis); this is done either with a strain gauge or by measuring the amount of light absorbed by the structure
- **skin conductance**; **skin conductance level** (SCL) is the general level of skin conductance associated with a particular situation; a **skin conductance response** (SCR) is a rapid change in skin conductance in response to a particular event; one application is the lie detector test

3. **Invasive Physiological and Pharmacological Methods**

- in most cases, laboratory animals serve as the subjects when invasive procedures are required to directly manipulate or measure the brain

a. **Stereotaxic Surgery** *(use Digital Image Archive Figure CH05F14.BMP)*
- the first step in many invasive biopsychology experiments is stereotaxic surgery
- the method employs a **stereotaxic atlas** and a **stereotaxic instrument** (head holder; electrode holder); the reference point is often **bregma** (the point where two main plates of the rat skull naturally fuse together)

b. **Lesion Methods**
- the **aspiration** method is often used to remove cortical tissue
- the **radio-frequency** (high-frequency) electrolytic lesion is the most common subcortical lesion; the tissue is destroyed by the heat of the current
- small **knife cuts** are often used for severing tracts *(use Digital Image Archive Figure CH05F15.BMP)*
- **cryogenic blockade** is like a reversible lesion; the tissue is temporarily cooled to the point that all neural activity in the vicinity of the probe stops *(use Digital Image Archive Figure CH05F16.BMP)*

c. **Electrical Stimulation**
- the effects of electrical stimulation are often opposite to those of a lesion to the same brain site
- electrical stimulation research is done prior to any lesioning

d. Electrical Recording Methods *(use Digital Image Archive Figure CH05F17.BMP)*

- **intracellular unit recording**
    - is a measure of changes in the **membrane potential** of a neuron over time; it requires that a **microelectrode** be positioned inside a neuron; all of the recording that was discussed in Chapter 4 is of this type
    - it is next to impossible to record intracellularly in a freely moving animal because it is difficult to keep the microelectrode inside the neuron

- **extracellular unit recording**
    - a microelectrode is positioned near a neuron; the signal is a series of spikes; each spike indicates an action potential from a nearby neuron; spikes of the same amplitude are assumed to come from the same neuron

- **multiple-unit recording**
    - multiple-unit recording provides an indication of the rate of firing in the general vicinity of the electrode tip; an electrode larger than a microelectrode picks up the action potentials from many nearby neurons
    - the signal is integrated so that the height of the curve indicates the number of action potentials in the vicinity per unit of time

- **invasive EEG recording**
    - implanted electrodes are used to record EEG in laboratory animals because scalp electrodes do not allow as clear or finite position recording

e. **Psychopharmacological Methods**

Drug Administration:
- routes of drug administration include IG, IP, IV, SC, IM
- these peripheral routes all suffer from the fact that many drugs cannot pass the blood-brain barrier; this problem can be overcome by administering drug via intraventricular cannula or by microinjection of drugs directly into brain tissue

Selective Chemical Lesions:

- **6-hydroxydopamine** (6-OHDA) is a neurotoxin that selectively destroys dopaminergic and noradrenergic neurons in the vicinity of the injection site
- **kainic acid** or **ibotenic acid** destroy neurons with cell bodies at the site of injection, but they leave axons passing through the area undamaged

Measuring the Chemical Activity of the Brain in Behavioral Experiments:

- **2-deoxyglucose autoradiography**
    - radioactive 2-DG is injected; then the animal performs the test activity of interest
    - the animal is immediately killed, its brain is removed and sliced, the slices are coated with a photographic emulsion, and finally after a few days in the dark, the areas of the brain that were particularly active during the test activity show up as dark spots of radioactivity; this procedure is called autoradiography

In Vivo **Cerebral Microdialysis**
- can be used to measure neurotransmitters and chemicals secreted by the neuron during synaptic transmission in behaving animals
- a fine U-shaped tube is inserted into the brain of an animal; a solution circulates through the tube
- at the tip, the tube is semipermeable so that chemicals are continuously drawn from the brain into the solution in the tube, where they are carried away for analysis

In Vivo Voltammetry
- changes in the concentrations of certain neurochemicals can be inferred from changes in flow of **current** across a carbon-based electrode as the voltage is gradually increased; these changes can be measured as the subject is engaged in various behaviors

Locating Neurotransmitters and Receptors in the Brain:

Immunocytochemistry:
- involves injecting **antigens** (foreign proteins) into an animal such that the animal will create and bind **antibodies** to the antigen to remove or destroy it
- antibodies for most of the brain's peptide neurotransmitters and receptors have been created, thus specific neuroproteins can be located by labeling   the antibodies and allowing antibodies to attach to the neuroproteins; brain tissue is then removed and sliced to reveal locations where labels have accumulated on neuroproteins

In Situ Hybridization:
- allows peptides and proteins in the brain to be located via obtaining hybrid RNA   strands with a base sequence complementary to the mRNA for synthesizing the target neuroprotein; labeling the hybrid RNA which then bind to complementary mRNA strands allows the target neuroprotein's location to be marked

4. Genetic Engineering

1. Gene Knockout Techniques:

- involve the creation of organisms that lack a specific gene; any measurable neural or behavioral anomalies are then noted
- PROBLEMS: 1) Most behaviors are **polymorphic traits**; 2) Eliminating one gene usually alters the expression of other genes; 3) gene expression is dependent upon experience, which may be altered by the absence of the missing gene; and 4) control subjects and knockout subjects have different DNA, due to the procedure used to create the knockout organism.

2. Gene Replacement Techniques:

- involves the replacement of one gene with another; useful implications for the treatment of genetically-related diseases.

- sometimes, genetic information from a different species is implanted, creating a **transgenic** subject.

Suggested Websites for Lecture 5a:

A Primer for CAT and MRI: *http://www.med.harvard.edu/AANLIB/hms1.html*

From Dr. Keith Johnston's Whole Brain Atlas, an explanation of CAT and MRI techniques. Very good.

The Electroencephalogram (EEG): *http://www.medfak.uu.se/fysiologi/Lectures/EEG.html*

A great page with basic information about EEGs and evoked potentials, and rudimentary information about the use of EEG in pathological conditions.

Neurochemistry in Freely-Moving Animals:

In vivo **Microdialysis:** *http://www.microdialysis.se/techniqu.htm*

From CMA, a basic description of the technique of in vivo microdialysis, used to measure neurochemical changes in conscious, freely moving animals. See also:

In vivo Voltammetry: *http://www.mds.qmw.ac.uk/anae/fcv.htm*

A basic description of fast cyclic voltammetry, one voltammetric technique used to monitor neurochemical changes in conscious, freely moving animals.

Every experiment is useful, even if it
is only to serve as a bad example

Lecture 5b

BEHAVIORAL RESEARCH METHODS OF BIOPSYCHOLOGY

Outline

1. Neuropsychological Testing
    a. General Intelligence
    b. Lateralization
    c. Memory
    d. Language
    e. Perceptual-Motor Function

2. Behavioral Methods of Cognitive Neuroscience
    a. Constituent Cognitive Processes Assumption
    b. Paired Image Subtraction Technique

3. Paradigms of Animal Behavior
    a. Analysis of Species-Common Behaviors
    b. Traditional Conditioning Paradigms
    c. Seminatural Animal Learning Paradigms

4. Conclusion: Converging Operations

Lecture Notes

1. **Neuropsychological Testing**

    -   methods used to assess psychological deficits of human patients suspected of having brain damage

    a. **General Intelligence:**
        -   most neuropsychological assessments begin with the **Wechsler Adult Intelligence Scale (WAIS)**
        -   it has 11 subtests; 6 comprise the **verbal scale** (e.g., Digit Span, Information, Similarities); 5 comprise the **performance scale** (e.g., block design, object assembly)

    b. **Lateralization:**
        -   evaluating the effects of damage to the right and left hemispheres
        -   the following two tests are well known tests of language lateralization
        -   **sodium amytal test**: sodium amytal is injected first into one **carotid artery** and then, many minutes later, into the other; the patient is mute following an injection ipsilateral to the dominant hemisphere for language; but the patient makes only a few minor speech errors after an injection contralateral to the dominant hemisphere for language
        -   **dichotic listening test:** it is a noninvasive test; three pairs of digits are presented to the subject through headphones; the two digits of each pair are presented simultaneously, one to each ear; the subjects are asked to report the six digits that they heard; they do slightly better through the ear contralateral to the hemisphere dominant for language

    c. **Memory**
        -   the WAIS **digit-span subtest** is the most common test of verbal short-term memory
        -   the WAIS **information test** (who is the president of the U.S.A.?) is a quick way of identifying gross deficits in long-term verbal memory; these can be adapted to an individual's culture
        -   a thorough assessment of the various types of memory requires several tests

d. **Language**
- the **token test** is a good initial screening test for language-related deficits; if the token test identifies deficits, it is followed up by a battery of tests of language ability
- there are 20 tokens of 2 different shapes, 2 different sizes, and 5 different colors; the subject is asked to carry out various acts such as "touch the small blue circle and then the large green square"

e. **Frontal Lobe Function**
- the **Wisconsin Card Sorting Test** is often used *(use Digital Image Archive Figure CH05F22.BMP)*
  - each card in the deck has 1, 2, 3, or 4 triangles, circles, squares, or crosses that are all red, green, yellow, or blue
  - the subject is told to sort the cards into four different piles but is not told on what basis the sorting is to be accomplished; they are told after each card is placed in a pile whether or not it was correctly placed
  - at first the patient must learn to sort by color, but once she or he has learned this sorting principle, the correct principle changes without warning to form or number
  - patients with **frontal-lobe lesions** adapt poorly to rule changes; they **perseverate** (they continue to respond in a previously correct fashion long after it has become incorrect)

2. **Behavioral Methods of Cognitive Neuroscience**

a. **constituent cognitive process assumption**
- refers to the premise that complex cognitive processes are the combined activity of simple cognitive processes and that each constituent cognitive process is mediated by neural activity in a particular area of the brain
- cognitive psychologists, computer scientists, and neuroscientists combine efforts to model complex cognitive   processes, for clinical as well as artificial intelligence applications

b. **paired-image subtraction techniques**
- are key to neuroscience research by examining PET or functional MRI images on tasks that differ in only one constituent cognitive process; the difference between the two images is thus viewed as specific to the one constituent cognitive process that was different between the two images
- processes such as seeing, reading, and speaking words are frequently used in this type of research

3. **Animal Behavior Paradigms**

a. **Analysis of Species-Common Behaviors**

- these behaviors are displayed in the same form by virtually all members of a species, of the same sex (e.g., grooming, swimming, nest building, copulating)

- the **open-field test** provides three measures of emotionality: (1) degree of inactivity, (2) **thigmotaxis**, and (3) defecation

- **aggression** and **defense** can be studied by recording encounters between a small male intruder and a colony's dominant (**alpha**) male; **aggression** involves a sideways approach, sideways pushing, piloerection, and biting directed at the back; defense involves boxing, rolling over onto the back, biting the face, freezing, and fleeing

- rat **sexual behavior** is another species-common behavior that is widely studied
- two common measures of female rat sexual receptivity are (1) **lordosis quotient** (proportion of mounts producing lordosis), and (2) degree of concavity of the back during lordosis
- male rat behaviors measured include number of **mounts** to **intromission**, number of intromissions to **ejaculation**, and time to reinitiate mounting after ejaculation (the **postejaculatory interval**)

b. **Traditional Conditioning Paradigms**

- traditional conditioning paradigms play an important role in biopsychology for two reasons:
  (1) conditioning is a phenomenon of primary interest to psychologists; and (2) conditioning
  procedures are often used to train laboratory animals to perform as required in behavioral
  experiments
- there are two kinds of traditional conditioning paradigms:
  1) **Pavlovian conditioning:** in which a neutral stimulus called a **conditional stimulus** (CS; e.g.,
     tone) is paired with an **unconditional stimulus** (US; e.g. meat powder) that elicits an
     unconditional response (UR; e.g. salivation). As the CS becomes associated with the US, it
     begins to elicit a response on its own which is referred to as a conditional response (CR). The
     CR is usually similar to the UR, but this is not always the case.
  2) **Operant Conditioning:** in which the rate of a particular response is increased by
     reinforcement or decreased by **punishment.**

c. **Seminatural Animal Learning Paradigms**

- **ethoexperimental** animal learning paradigms are controlled laboratory paradigms for studying
  forms of learning that are assumed to occur in the rat's natural environment; the following are four
  examples:

1) **Conditioned Taste Aversion:**
- the most influential ethoexperimental learning paradigm; rats and many other animals learn the
  relation between a new taste and subsequent gastrointestinal distress in one trial and subsequently
  avoid the novel taste
- taste aversion conditioning experiments in the 1960s challenged three widely held views of learning
  that had grown out of the study of the traditional conditioning paradigms: (1) the view that learning
  is a gradual **step-by-step process** by showing that it could occur reliably in one trial, (2) the view
  that **temporal contiguity** is necessary for learning by showing that conditioning occurred even
  when the taste and distress were separated by several hours, and (3) the view that associations
  between any two stimuli are equally easy to learn (the **principle of equipotentiality**) by showing
  that rats could learn the relation between gastrointestinal distress and a taste, but not a light

2) **Radial-Arm Maze:** *(use Digital Image Archive Figure CH05F25.BMP)*
- is used to study foraging behavior in the laboratory
- foraging in the wild is complex; the rat must learn where food is likely to be, but not to immediately
  revisit a stripped site
- in the radial-arm maze rats quickly learn to go directly to the arms that are baited with food each
  day, but they rarely visit the same arm twice on a given trial

3) **Morris Water Maze:**
- is another laboratory paradigm used to study rat spatial ability; the Morris water maze is a large tub
  of milky water; to get out of the water, rats must learn to swim to a slightly submerged (invisible)
  goal platform
- rats learn to do this very quickly, even when they are placed in the water at a different position on
  each trial; they use external room cues to guide them
- it is interesting to look at their search strategies when the platform has been moved to a new
  location

4) **Conditioned Defensive Burying:**
- based on observation that rats exposed to an inanimate object that has been the source of a single
  aversive stimulus (e.g., a shock, a bad odor, an airblast, or a flash) will often bury it
- they bury it by facing it and spraying bedding or sand at it with their head and forelegs
- it has been used to study antianxiety drug effects; antianxiety drugs reduce conditioned defensive
  burying at low doses

4.   Conclusion: Converging Operations

- you have now learned about many research methods used by biopsychologists; they all have strengths, but they all have weaknesses
- the key to scientific progress lies in **converging operations** (bringing several methods to bear on the same problem so that each compensates for the shortcomings of the others)

Suggested Websites for Lecture 5b:

The Wechsler Intelligence Scales: *http://www.richmond.edu/~capc/wechsler page.html*

> A page focusing on the Wechsler Intelligence scales, including a history of the WAIS, its subscales, and the WISC.   See the Pros and Cons section for high (and low) points of these scales.

Virtual Operant Conditioning: *http://www.thecroft.com/psy/op.rat.html*

> Website for OpRat, software that allows students to study the operant behavior of a virtual rat. Downloadable software is available, although the full version of the software is only available commercially.

Why Study Animal Behavior? *http://www.animalbehavior.org/ABS/Education/valueofanimalbehavior.html*

> From Dr. Charles Snowdon, a past president of the Animal Behavior Society; thoughtful essay on the value of basic and applied animal research.

Experiments in Cognitive Psychology: *http://www.psych.purdue.edu/~coglab/demos.html*

> From Purdue University's Cognitive Psychology group, a collection of experiments useful for lab instruction or simply a better understanding of some basic phenomena in the area.

Lecture 6a

NEUROPSYCHOLOGICAL DISORDERS

Outline

1. Causes and Effects of Brain Damage
   a. Tumors
   b. Cerebrovascular Disorders
   c. Closed-Head Injuries
   d. Infections
   e. Neurotoxins
   f. Genetic Factors

2. Epilepsy
   a. Partial Seizures
   b. Generalized Seizures

3. Parkinson's Disease

4. Huntington's Disease

5. Multiple Sclerosis

6. Alzheimer's Disease

Lecture Notes

1. Causes and Effects of Brain Damage:

- much can be learned about the brain's normal functioning by examining deficits after brain damage

a. Tumors
   - a tumor (neoplasm) is a group of cells growing independently of the rest of the body; a tumor can be **encapsulated** or **infiltrating**; it can be **benign** or **malignant**
   - **metastatic tumors** are tumors that originate in one organ and spread to another; the symptoms of multiple cerebral tumors are often the first signs of lung cancer
   - 20% of brain tumors are **meningiomas** that grow in the meninges; they are encapsulated and benign

b. Cerebrovascular Disorders
   - "**stroke**" is commonly used to refer to any cerebrovascular disorder of sudden onset
   - **intracerebral hemorrhage**; the bursting of **aneurysms** (balloon-like dilations of weak areas of blood vessels) is a major cause of intracerebral bleeding; aneurysms can be **congenital** or the result of infection, toxins etc.
   - **cerebral ischemia** is cell death caused by interruption of blood supply to an area of the brain; cells die from a shortage of oxygen (**hypoxia**); the area of damage is called an **infarct**. There are three main causes of cerebral ischemia:

     (1) in **thrombosis** a plug (a **thrombus**) becomes lodged at its site of formation; the plug may comprise hair, oil, cancerous cells, air bubbles, etc.;
     (2) in **embolism** a plug (an **embolus**) travels from its site of formation and becomes lodged in a smaller blood vessel; and
     (3) in **arteriosclerosis** the thickening of a blood vessel wall, usually from the accumulation of fat, blocks blood flow

- the role of **excitatory amino acids** in stroke-produced brain damage is currently under investigation *(use Digital Image Archive Figure CH06F04.bmp)*
- **glutamate,** the brain's most prevalent excitatory amino acid neurotransmitter is released in excessive quantities when blood vessels are blocked and deprive neurons of nutrients
- the excessive glutamate overactivates glutamate receptors on postsynaptic membrane sites thus too many Na+ and Ca++ ions are allowed to enter the postsynaptic neuron; the over abundance of Na+ and Ca++ triggers either (a) an excessive release of glutamate, causing a cascade of this toxic effect or, (b) triggers a sequence of reactions that kills the postsynaptic neuron
- in experimental animals, **NMDA receptor blockers** administered directly after a stroke have been shown to reduce subsequent brain damage

c. Closed-head Injuries
- a brain **contusion** is an injury in which there is bleeding from the blow in the absence of a **laceration;** the bleeding results in a **hematoma** (a bruise or collection of clotted blood); contusions are caused by the brain hitting the skull, and they are often *contre coup* (on other side of brain from blow)
- **concussion** is the diagnosis when a blow to the head disrupts consciousness, but no evidence of physical damage can be found; the **punch-drunk syndrome** is the general dementia due to an accumulation of many concussions

d. Infections
- **encephalitis** is the general term for inflammation of the brain resulting from infection
- **bacterial infections** can be treated with antibiotics, but if left untreated they can cause **meningitis** (inflammation of meninges), **brain abscesses** (pockets of pus), and **general paresis** (from syphilis bacteria)
- **viral infections** cannot be successfully treated; **neurotropic** viral brain infections preferentially attack the nervous system (e.g., rabies virus); **pantropic** viral brain infections show no preference for the nervous system but they sometimes attack it (e.g., mumps and herpes viruses)

e. Neurotoxins
- brain damage can be produced by a variety of toxins in the environment; "mad hatters" were the result of **mercury poisoning**; "crackpots" were originally those who drank tea from cracked ceramic pots with **lead** cores; the result was poisoning
- **exogenous** vs. **endogenous** toxins; in autoimmune disorders toxins appear to be created by the patient's own body; e.g., in **multiple sclerosis** the patient seems to manufacture antibodies to his or her own myelin impairing neural transmission

f. Genetic Factors
- some genetic disorders are accidents of cell division; e.g., in **Down syndrome** an extra chromosome in pair 21 is present in all cells
- more commonly, genetic disorders are products of abnormal genes; strong evidence that a disorder is the product of abnormal genes comes from twin studies (**monozygotic** vs. **dizygotic**) and from early-adoption studies
- the situation is more complex when what is inherited is a hypersusceptibility to some other agent (e.g., an infection or toxin); e.g., in **phenylketonuria** the patient inherits no enzyme to metabolize the amino acid **phenylalanine** and is poisoned by phenylalanine-rich diets
- genetic neuropsychological disorders are usually associated with recessive genes; otherwise, the organism would not survive to pass them on to its progeny. However, there are cases where a dominant gene is abnormal; the most notable is **Huntington's disease,** a motor disease that does not develop until a person is likely to have had children.

g. Programmed Cell Death

- dysfunctional neurons and other cells are eliminated by activating genes that kill them; this programmed cell death is called **apoptosis.** This differs from **necrosis,** in which neurons die passively as a result of injury.

2. **Epilepsy** *(use Digital Image Archive Figure CH06F07.bmp)*
   - epilepsy is any disorder in which epileptic seizures recur **spontaneously**
   - when **convulsions** (motor seizures) are present, epilepsy is easy to diagnose; convulsions often involve **clonus** (tremor), **tonus** (rigidity), loss of balance, and/or loss of consciousness
   - however, many seizures involve subtle changes in thought, mood, and/or behavior with no convulsive symptoms whatsoever
   - the observation of **epileptic spikes** in the EEG is incontrovertible evidence of epilepsy; however, failure to observe them does not prove that the person is not epileptic
   - there are two main classes of seizures: **partial seizures** and **generalized seizures**

   a. Partial Seizures

      - partial seizures are those that do not involve the entire brain
      - **simple partial seizures** are partial seizures whose symptoms are primarily sensory and/or motor; usually the symptoms start in one part of the body and spread through it as discharges spread through the sensory and motor areas of the brain
      - **complex partial seizures** are characterized by psychological and behavioral symptoms that look much like normal behaviors; they often begin with a complex psychological symptom called an **aura** (an idea, a memory, a visual, auditory or olfactory signal, an emotion, etc.), which may or may not develop into motor symptoms; the motor symptoms of complex partial seizures vary in complexity from **automatisms** (simple, compulsive, repeated behaviors such as tugging on a piece of hair) to **psychomotor attacks** (long sequences of behavior that are out of context and slightly peculiar but are, for the most part, normal-appearing); epileptics typically have no memory for the events of a complex partial seizure

   b. Generalized Seizures

      - generalized seizures are those that involve the entire brain; they may start from a **focus** and gradually spread, or they may begin almost simultaneously throughout the entire brain; for example, **grand mal seizures** ("big trouble") (**tonic-clonic**, loss of balance and consciousness, tongue biting, **incontinence**, turning blue from **hypoxia**) and **petit mal seizures** ("little trouble") (petit mal absence, 3-per-second spike-and-wave; *(use Digital Image Archive Figure CH06F09.bmp)*

3. **Parkinson's Disease**

   - Parkinson's disease attacks 0.5% of the population; it usually develops in people in their 50s or 60s; the first symptom is often a tremor or stiffness of the fingers (the same symptoms seen in many other long- and short-term disorders)
   - symptoms of the full-blown disorder are **tremor at rest**, muscular rigidity, **cruel restlessness**, **bradykinesia** (poverty and slowness of movement), and a shuffling, wide-based gait; there is no intellectual deterioration (no **dementia**)
   - its cause is unknown, but it is associated with degeneration in the **dopamine** pathway from the **substantia nigra** to the **striatum**; treated with **L-DOPA** because dopamine does not readily penetrate the blood-brain barrier; **Deprenyl**, an **MAO inhibitor** dopamine agonist, slows the development of the disorder

4. **Huntington's Disease**

   - like Parkinson's disease, it is a motor disorder; unlike Parkinson's disease, it is inherited but rare, its cause is understood, and it is always associated with **dementia**
   - its main symptoms are complex jerky movements of entire limbs; because the movements in some cases are dance-like, it was called **Huntington's chorea** ("dance like")
   - Huntington's disease is caused by a single **dominant gene**; 50% of all offspring of a Huntington's parent will get it; the reason the disease has not disappeared is that the first symptoms do not appear until after the age of reproduction (at 40-50 years of age); the patient dies about 15 years after the first symptoms appear
   - it is now possible to test the sons and daughters of a Huntington's parent to determine which have inherited the lethal gene; would you want such a test if you were in such a situation?

5. Multiple Sclerosis

- MS is a disease of CNS **myelin;** it leads to the development of areas of hard scar tissue throughout the CNS; "sclerosis" means "hardening"
- the symptoms depend on the location of the scars; but common symptoms are **ataxia** (loss of motor coordination), weakness, numbness, tremor, and poor vision
- it attacks people in early adulthood; there are often periods of partial recovery, but there are no exceptions to the generally worsening progression of the disorder
- it is more common in cool climates; it is rare among orientals; the concordance rate is 36% in **monozygotic** twins and 12% in **dizygotic** twins; thus there are heredity and environmental factors
- because a similar disorder (**experimental allergic encephalomyelitis**) can be produced in animals by injecting them with myelin and a substance that stimulates the body's immune reaction, it is believed that MS results from a faulty immune reaction against the body's own myelin, perhaps resulting from an early infection or toxin

6. Alzheimer's Disease (use Digital Image Archive Figure CH06F12.bmp)

- 3% of people over 65 and 10% over 85 years old suffer from Alzheimer's disease; the first signs (in those as young as 40) are a decline in cognitive ability (e.g. forgetfulness) and emotional instability (e.g. depression); eventually there is total **dementia** and an inability to perform even the most simple responses (e.g., swallowing); it is **terminal**
- autopsy reveals: (1) loss of neurons (particularly cholinergic neurons), (2) **amyloid plaques** (clumps of degenerating neurons next to an abnormal protein called **amyloid**), and (3) tangles of **neurofibrils** within neurons
- in one study (using subjects with an early onset form of Alzheimer's disease that runs through families) the abnormal gene was identified; it was on **chromosome 21,** the same chromosome involved **in Down's syndrome**; Down's patients that survive until adulthood almost always develop Alzheimer's disease

Suggested Websites for Lecture 6a:

Brain Trauma: *http://coconet03.coconet.com/~neuroblade/z-brain.html*

From the Neurosurgeon site maintained by Michael Lusk, MD, a collection of pages and links related to head trauma and surgery. Includes a glossary of neurosurgical terms as well as images and brief text of various sorts of cerebral trauma, with links to many other sites related to stroke, traumatic head injury, aneurysms, and other cerebral disorders. See also:

http://www.med.harvard.edu/AANLIB/

for the Whole Brain Atlas site and some excellent images and time-lapse movies of various brain trauma, including stroke, Alzheimer's disease, Huntington's disease, and MS.

Huntington's Disease: *http://neuro-www2.mgh.harvard.edu/hdsa/hdsamain.nclk*

From the Huntington's Disease Society of America, a good resource for those interested in the etiolgy and cause of HD.

Parkinson's Disease:

http://medweb.bham.ac.uk/http/depts/clin_neuro/teaching/tutorials/parkinsons/parkinsons1.html

An abysmally long URL, but a great site from the Department of Clinical Neurosciences at the University of Birmingham, England; note the references to James Parkinson's original monograph, the links to the anatomical correlates of Parkinson's Disease, and the QuickTime movies of patients displaying the symptoms of Parkinson's Disease.

Lecture 6b

ANIMAL MODELS OF HUMAN NEUROPSYCHOLOGICAL DISORDERS

Outline

1. What is an animal model?

2. Kindling Model of Epilepsy

3. Transgenic Mouse Model of Alzheimer's Disease

4. MPTP Model of Parkinson's Disease

Lecture Notes

1. What is an animal model?

- it is rare that the type of **experiments** necessary to understand a human neuropsychological disorder can be conducted on human patients; **quasiexperimental studies** may be possible, but not experiments; thus it is difficult to study the causal factors in human neuropsychological disorders
- accordingly, the study of **animal models** has contributed much to the understanding of some neuropsychological disorders
- the decision to induce a neuropsychological disorder in a laboratory animal is not a decision that is made lightly; the medical researcher must make difficult decisions such as to engage in research that involves the induction of pathological states in laboratory animals, or to potentially contribute to the suffering and death of untold thousands of humans by refusing to engage in a line of research that might eventually lead to an effective new treatment
- there are three kinds of animal models:

    - **homologous animal models** are animal disorders that duplicate the human disorder in every significant respect (**etiology**, underlying pathology, symptoms, and **prognosis**)

    - **isomorphic animal models** are animal disorders that duplicate the human disorder in every significant respect, but are induced in the laboratory in a way that does not resemble the etiology of the human disorder

    - **predictive animal models** do not closely resemble the human disorder in any obvious way, but there is something about the model that allows the researcher to make predictions about the human disorder or its response to treatment

- to use an animal model one must appreciate what kind of model it is; e.g., etiology cannot be studied with isomorphic and predictive models, and the underlying physiological pathology cannot be identified with a predictive model; truly homologous models of nervous system disorders are rare; at best animal models model only some aspects of a disorder
- the problem in developing an animal model is that it is often not possible to tell how well an animal model equates to the human disorder because we don't have a complete understanding of the human disorder; this is a classic "Catch 22" situation

2. Kindling Model of Epilepsy

- in the typical kindling experiment, an animal (usually a rat) receives one mild brief (usually 1 second) electrical stimulation (usually to the amygdala) at regular intervals (usually once per day)
- the first stimulation has no behavioral effect; however, after a few stimulations a mild convulsion involving clonic jaw movements is elicited; with further stimulation the convulsions elicited by each stimulation become longer and longer and more and more **generalized**; after about 15 amygdala stimulations, each stimulation produces a fully generalized convulsion (characterized in sequence by jaw clonus, head nodding, forelimb clonus, rearing up, and falling)
- kindling can be produced by the periodic stimulation of many brain sites other than the amygdala, and it can also be produced by the periodic injection of initially subconvulsive doses of convulsive drugs-- although the form of the convulsions is different for different agents
- kindling has been reported in many species other than rats (e.g., frogs, rabbits, mice, cats, dogs, monkeys, baboons)
- kindling does not occur at all at short interstimulation intervals (less than 20 minutes or so); and it takes many more stimulations to kindle if the intervals are less than an hour or so
- the most interesting and important aspect of kindling is its permanence; if an animal is kindled and then left unstimulated for several weeks, the next stimulation often elicits a generalized convulsion; thus the change in the brain that underlies kindling does not go away when the series of stimulations is curtailed
- the kindling paradigm has been used as a model in two ways:

   1) kindling has been used as a model of **epileptogenesis** (the development of epilepsy); many researchers feel that if they discover the mechanism of kindling, they will discover changes that turn a healthy human into an epileptic; drugs that block kindling, may prove to be effective **prophylactically** against the development of epilepsy (e.g., against the epilepsy that sometimes develops after a blow to the head)

   2) the convulsions elicited in kindled rats by stimulation of various areas have been used as models of clinical convulsions; many studies have used kindled convulsions to test the effectiveness of anticonvulsant drugs; for example, Racine et al., (1975) found that **diphenylhydantoin (Dilantin)** blocked kindled convulsions elicited by **neocortical** stimulation but not those elicited by amygdala stimulation; **diazepam (Valium)** did not block neocortical convulsions but did block amygdalar convulsions

- kindled convulsions as studied in most labs are not isomorphic models of epilepsy; in epilepsy, convulsions recur spontaneously, whereas kindled convulsions are elicited; however, experiments on rats by Pinel and on monkeys, baboons, and cats by Wada have shown that if animals are kindled long enough (e.g., 300 stimulations in rats), they will eventually become truly epileptic; they will have convulsions that recur spontaneously even after the stimulations have been curtailed

3. Transgenic Mouse Model of Alzheimer's Disease

- the most exciting advance in Alheimer's disease research in many years; area has suffered for lack of a good animal model
- in the most promising transgenic mouse model, genes that accelerate human amyloid development are injected into fertilized mouse embryos
- as mice mature, their brains develop amyloid plaques with a distribution similar to that seen in human patients.
- more importantly, these transgenic mice also display deficits on various tasks of learning and memory, much like their human counterparts.

4. MPTP Model of Parkinson's Disease

- we discussed Parkinson's disease last day; the symptoms are tremor at rest, muscular rigidity, cruel restlessness, poverty and slowness of movement, and shuffling wide-based gait; Parkinson patients are typically intellectually normal
- in 1982, several young people were admitted to hospital with severe Parkinson's symptoms; this was surprising because such severe cases are not usually seen before the age of 50
- it was discovered that all were opiate addicts who had recently used an illicit synthetic opiate made by the same person; some of the batch was obtained, and it was found to contain 1-methyl-4-phenyl-1,2,3,6-tetrahydropyridine or **MPTP**
- the similarity between the MPTP syndrome and Parkinson's disease was remarkable; even minor symptoms of Parkinson's disease such as **seborrhea** (oily skin) and **micrographia** (very small handwriting) were present
- this suggested that Parkinson's disease might be effectively studied in an MPTP animal model; it was quickly established that laboratory primates exposed to MPTP reacted similarly; they displayed similar behavioral symptoms and similar neural pathology; there was cell loss in the **substantia nigra** and a reduction in **dopamine**
- curiously, the behavioral effects of MPTP on laboratory rodents proved to be mild, unreliable, and temporary; also, some MPTP monkeys do not develop the parkinsonian symptoms even though their dopamine is depleted
- you will learn in Chapter 15 that the MPTP animal model has played a major role in the development of the exciting new neurotransplantation treatment for Parkinson's disease
- MPTP animal modeling has also led to the discovery that **deprenyl**, a monoamine agonist and monoamine oxidase (MAO) inhibitor acts to block the effects of MPTP by increasing the level of dopamine via the inhibition of monoamine oxidase; deprenyl administration in early Parkinson's patients greatly slows the progression of the disease

Suggested Websites for Lecture 6b:

Animal Models of Parkinson's Disease: *http://darwin.apnet.com/inscight/09301997/grapha.htm*

News on a genetically engineered mouse that resists the pathology associated with Parkinson's Disease.

Squirrels and Strokes: *http://www.sciencenews.org/sn_arc97/12_6_97/bob1.htm*

Insights that hibernating squirrels are giving stroke researchers about cerebral blood flow and brain function.

Lecture 7a

THE VISUAL SYSTEM: EYE TO CORTEX

Outline

1. The Eyes
   a. Structure
   b. Accommodation
   c. Binocular Disparity

2. The Retinas
   a. Structure
   b. Completion
   c. Duplexity Theory
   d. Eye Movements

3. Transduction by Rhodopsin

4. The Major Visual Pathway

Lecture Notes

1. The Eyes:

- vision is the most studied of the senses

   a. Structure: *(use Digital Image Archive Figure CH07F03.bmp)*
      - review the major structures of the eye.

   b. Accommodation
      - **ciliary muscles** adjust the lenses to focus visual images sharply on the retinas, regardless of their distance from the eyes; this focusing of the lenses is called **accommodation**
      - when we look at something near, the ciliary muscles contract, tension on the lenses is reduced, and they become more cylindrical
   c. Binocular Disparity
      - unlike most vertebrates, most mammals have two eyes on the front of their heads, rather than one on each side; this cuts down the field of view, but it insures that most of what is seen is seen through both eyes
      - because each eye sees things from a slightly different perspective, there is a difference in the two retinal images; this **binocular disparity** is greater for closer things; the degree of binocular disparity associated with a particular visual stimulus helps the brain create a 3-dimensional perception from two 2-dimensional retinal images thus depth perception is achieved

2. The Retinas

   a. Structure *(use Digital Image Archive Figure CH07F04.bmp)*
      - five layers: (1) receptor layer, (2) horizontal cell layer, (3) bipolar layer, (4) amacrine cell layer, (5) retinal ganglion cell layer
      - the receptor layer is the farthest of the layers from light; therefore, incoming light is distorted by four layers of neurons before reaching the receptors

- the **fovea** is a pit about 330 μ in diameter; it is the only part of the retina capable of mediating high-acuity vision. This is due, in part, to the fact that axons of the retinal ganglion cells are thinnest over the fovea and light is distorted less before reaching the layer of receptors. The fovea is roughly in the center of your field of vision, which is why you tend to hold tasks that require a high degree of acuity (e.g., threading a needle) in the center of your visual field.
- the **optic disk** is where the axons of retinal ganglion cells penetrate the retina and exit the eye; the optic disk has no receptors thus creating a **blind spot**

b. Completion
   - we all have a blind spot at the optic disk, due to the exit of axons from the retinal ganglion cells
   - we are normally unaware of our blind spots, even when looking through one stationary eye, because of **completion;** the visual system is able to use visual information gathered from receptors around the optic disk to "complete" the visual image
   - completion illustrates the creativity of the visual system

c. Duplexity Theory
   - in a sense, each of us has two visual systems; the **photopic** system functions in lighted conditions; the **scotopic** system functions in dim light
   - cones mediate photopic vision; rods mediate scotopic vision
   - the photopic system mediates **high-acuity** vision; the scotopic system mediates **low-acuity** vision
   - the photopic system has **low sensitivity** with few receptors' information combined at the next cell level **(low convergence)** *(use Digital Image Archive Figure CH07F07.bmp)*
   - the scotopic system has **high sensitivity** with many receptors converging on ganglion cells (**high convergence**) *(use Digital Image Archive Figure CH07F07.bmp)*
   - only cones are in the fovea; rods predominate in the periphery

d. Eye Movements
   - our eyes are in continual motion; they make a series of **fixations** (about 3 per second) connected by **saccades** (rapid movements between fixations)
   - eye movements keep the visual image in continual motion on the retina; the importance of this movement is illustrated by the fact that **stabilized retinal images** disappear; most visual system neurons respond to change, not to steady input
   - what we perceive at any instance is the sum of the input that has been received during the last few fixations; this **temporal integration** of retinal images explains why our visual images are detailed, colored, and wide-angled, despite the small size of the fovea; it also explains why things don't disappear when we blink

3. **Transduction by Rhodopsin**

   - **transduction** is the conversion of one form of energy to another; the first step in visual transduction is conversion of light to neural signals by the rods and cones
   - transduction by rods is well understood; there is a pink substance in rods called **rhodopsin**; light is absorbed by **rhodopsin,** and this **bleaches** it (removes its color); this bleaching occurs because **retinal** and **opsin,** the two components of rhodopsin, separate in light
   - this bleaching reaction **hyperpolarizes** the rods, thus the bleaching reaction transduces light to a cascade of intracellular events resulting in a neural signal
   - when rhodopsin is totally bleached by intense light, rods lose their ability to absorb light and transduce; however, in the dark, retinal and opsin are reunited, and rhodopsin regains its color and its ability to absorb light and transduce
   - strong evidence that the absorption of light by rhodopsin is the first step in scotopic vision is the correspondence between rhodopsin's **absorption spectrum** and the scotopic spectral sensitivity curve

52

- rhodopsin is a G-protein linked receptor that responds to light by initiating a cascade of intracellular chemical events *(use Digital Image Archive Figure CH07F11.bmp)*
  - **cyclic GMP** is an intracellular chemical that keeps Na+ channels partly open when rods are in darkness; rods are thus slightly **depolarized**
  - bleaching rods via exposure to light results in an intracellular cascade of events that deactivates cyclic GMP, closing Na+ channels, which **hyperpolarizes** the rod and reduces the release of glutamate
  - rods thus transmit signals through the neural system via inhibition

4. The Major Visual Pathway *(use Digital Image Archive Figure CH07F12.bmp)*

- this is called the **retina-geniculate-striate pathway**
- the primary visual cortex is called **striate cortex** after the stripe seen in a Nissl-stained cross section of **lower layer IV**; the stripe is composed of the terminals of axons from the lateral geniculate nuclei
- the retinal ganglion cell axons from the **nasal hemiretinas** decussate via the **optic chiasm** (they are contralateral); those from the **temporal hemiretinas** remain **ipsilateral** providing redundancy for the system
- the most important feature of visual cortex organization is its **retinotopic** layout; the surface of the visual cortex is a map of the retina; as a result, when Dobelle et al., (1974) stimulated the brains of patients, who were blind from peripheral damage, through an array of electrodes, the patients saw a pattern of light that corresponded to the pattern on the cortex of electrodes that were simultaneously activated; if the activated electrodes were in an "X" shape, the patient saw an "X" although the organization in the visual cortex is inverted and reversed
- the **retina-geniculate-striate system** includes two largely independent channels: the P pathway and the M pathway

  1) **Parvocellular layers** (P layers) are found in the top four layers of each lateral geniculate nucleus (LGN) and are composed of small body neurons (parvo means "small"); they are responsive to color, fine detail patterns, and react to slow or stationary objects
  2) **Magnocellular layers** (M layers) are found in the bottom two layers of the LGN, composed of large body neurons (magno means "large"), and are responsive to rods and movement

Suggest Websites for Lecture 7a:

Everything You Could Need to Know about the Vertebrate Retina:
http://insight.med.utah.edu/Webvision/index.html

From Helga Kolb, Eduardo Fernandez, and Ralph Nelson at the University of Utah...an exhaustive list of the anatomy and physiology of the vertebrate retina. For advanced students and faculty.

First Stages of Vision: *http://www.accessexcellence.org/AE/AEC/CC/vision_background.html*

From Genentech's Access Excellence site, a comprehensive yet accessible review of the anatomy and physiology of the eye.

Retinal Implants: *http://rleweb.mit.edu/retina/*

A joint project of Harvard and MIT, one of several groups world-wide that are striving to perfect electronic retinal prostheses for people suffering from degenerative retinal diseases.

Gross Anatomy of the Visual System: *http://www9.biostr.washington.edu/da.html*

From the Digital Anatomist Project at the University of Washington; select the Interactive Brain Atlas and then look at the 3-D Pathways, Optic Radiations for a reconstruction of the visual system from retina to occipital lobe.

Lecture 7b

THE PERCEPTION OF CONTRAST AND ITS NEURAL BASIS

Outline

1. Contrast: The Perception of Edges

2. Lateral Inhibition: The Physiological Basis of Contrast Enhancement

3. Brightness-Contrast Detectors in the Mammalian Visual System
   a. Mapping Receptive Fields
   b. Receptive Fields of Neurons in the Retina-Geniculate-Striate Pathway
   c. Simple Cortical Cells
   d. Complex Cortical Cells
   e. Hubel and Wiesel's Model of Striate-Cortex Organization

4. Seeing Color
   a. Component Theory
   b. Opponent Process Theory
   c. Color Constancy

Lecture Notes

1. **Contrast: The Perception of Edges**
   - edges are the most important stimuli in our visual world; they define the position and extent of things
   - edge perception is the perception of a contrast between two adjacent areas of the visual field; this lecture will focus on how the visual system controls **brightness contrast**

2. **Lateral Inhibition: The Physiological Basis of Contrast Enhancement**
   - **Mach bands** *(use Digital Image Archive Figure CH07F13.bmp)* are the result of contrast enhancement
   - the perception of edges is so important that there is a mechanism in the visual system that enhances our perception of brightness contrast; this is called **contrast enhancement**; thus what we see is even better than the physical reality
   - the mechanisms of contrast enhancement were studied in the eye of the horseshoe crab because of its simplicity; it is a simple compound eye, with each of its individual receptors (**ommatidia**) connected by a lateral neural network (the **lateral plexus**) *(use Digital Image Archive Figure CH07F14.bmp)*
   - when an ommatidium is activated, it inhibits its neighbors via the lateral plexus; contrast enhancement occurs because receptors near an edge on the dimmer side receive **more lateral inhibition** than receptors on the dimmer side further away from the edge while receptors near the edge on the brighter side receive **less lateral inhibition** than the receptors on the brighter further away from the edge

3. Brightness-Contrast Detectors in the Mammalian Visual System
   a. Mapping Receptive Fields
      - in the late 1950s, Hubel and Wiesel developed a method that became the standard method for studying visual system neurons
      - visual stimuli are presented on a screen in front of a **curarized** subject (usually a cat or a monkey); the image is artificially focused on the retina by an adjustable lens in front of the eye (because the **ciliary muscles** are curarized)
      - once an extracellular electrode is positioned in the neural structure of interest so that it is recording the action potentials of only one neuron, the neuron's receptive field is mapped; the **receptive field** of a neuron is the area of the visual field within which **appropriate visual stimuli** can influence the firing of that neuron
      - once the receptive field is defined, the task is to discover what particular stimuli presented within the field are most effective in changing the cell's firing

b. **Receptive Fields of Neurons in the Retina-Geniculate-Striate Pathway**
   - most **retinal ganglion cells, lateral geniculate nucleus neurons**, and the neurons in **lower layer IV** of the striate cortex have similar receptive fields
   - visual system neurons display **two patterns of responding**:

   (1) **on firing**;   (2) inhibition followed by **off firing**
   (use Digital Image Archive Figure CH07F14.bmp and Figure CH07F16.bmp)

   - the most effective way to influence the firing of these neurons is to fully illuminate only the "**on area**" or the "**off area**" of its receptive field; if one light is shone in the "on area" and one is simultaneously shone in the "off area", their effects cancel one another out by lateral inhibition; these neurons respond little to diffuse light
   - in effect, many neurons of the retina-geniculate-striate pathway respond to brightness contrast between the centers and peripheries of their visual fields
   - all neurons of the retina-geniculate-striate pathway are **monocular**; thus they respond to light in only one of the eye's visual fields

c. **Simple Cortical Cells**

   - simple cortical cells in the striate cortex have receptive fields like those that were just described, except that the two areas of the receptive fields are divided by straight lines
   - these cells respond best to bars or edges of light in a particular location in the receptive field and in a particular orientation (e.g., 45°)
   - all simple cells are **monocular**

d. **Complex Cortical Cells**

   - most of the cells in the striate cortex are **complex cells**; they are more numerous but are like simple cells in that they respond best to straight-line stimuli in a particular orientation; they are not responsive to diffuse light
   - complex cells are unlike simple cells in that the position of the stimulus within the receptive field does not matter; the cell responds to the appropriate stimulus no matter where it is in its large receptive field
   - over half of the complex cells are **binocular**, and about half of those that are binocular display **ocular dominance**

e. **Hubel and Wiesel's Model of Striate-Cortex Organization** *(to review use Digital Image Archive Figure CH07F21.bmp and Figure CH07F14.bmp)*

   - use *Digital Image Archive Figure CH07F18.bmp* to review electrophysiological evidence of the organization of the visual cortex:

     - **vertical electrode passes** find: (1) cells with receptive fields in the same part of the receptive field, (2) simple and complex, cells that all prefer the same orientation, and (3) binocular complex cells that are all dominated by the same eye (if they display ocular dominance)

     - during **horizontal electrode passes**: (1) receptive field location shifts slightly with each electrode advance, (2) orientation preference shifts slightly with each electrode advance, (3) ocular dominance periodically shifts to the other eye with electrode advances

   - **ocular dominance columns** can be visualized by injecting a large dose of **radioactive amino acid** in one eye, waiting several days, and then subjecting the cortex to **autoradiography**; ocular dominance columns are clearly visible in lower layer IV as alternating patches of radioactivity and nonradioactivity (see Figure 7.19 of BIOPSYCHOLOGY)

- columns of vertical-line-preferring neurons have been visualized by injecting **radioactive 2-DG** and then moving vertical stripes back and forth in front of the animal for 45 min.; the subjects were then immediately killed and their brains sectioned; columns of radioactivity were visible through all layers of striate cortex except lower layer IV (see Figure 7.20 of BIOPSYCHOLOGY)

4. **Seeing Color**

    a.   **Component Theory** *(use Digital Image Archive Figure CH07F26.bmp)*
- also called **trichromatic theory**; component processing occurs at the receptor level
- one of three different enzymes coats each cone; each enzyme reacts optimally to a spectrum of electromagnetic energy (color); the ratio of cones in each spectrum stimulated allows a summed stimulus and thus color differentiation

    b.   **Opponent Process Theory** *(use Digital Image Archive Figure CH07F26.bmp)*
- opponent processing occurs at all levels of the visual system beyond the receptors
- red-green and blue-yellow opponent cells fire in response to input from cones; when red cells are "on" one cannot see green and when yellow cells are "on" one cannot see blue

    c.   **Color Constancy**
- this is the tendency for an object to be perceived as the same color despite major changes in wavelengths of light that it reflects
- perception of color constancy allows objects to be distinguished in a memorable way
- Land demonstrated in his 1977 experiments that the color of objects is not a simple relationship with the wavelength being reflected but depends partly on the light reflected by surfaces surrounding the objects (see the demonstration in chapter 7 of BIOPSYCHOLOGY)
- Land's **retinex theory of color vision** follows the premise that the color of an object is determined by its reflectance and the visual system calculates the reflectance of surfaces by comparing the ability of a surface to absorb light in the three bandwidths corresponding to the three classes of cones
- **dual-opponent cells** provide the means to analyze contrast between wavelengths reflected by adjacent areas of their receptive fields

Suggested Websites for Lecture 7b:

On-Line Illusions and other Visual Phenomena: *http://weber.u.washington.edu/~chudler/chvision.html*

    A great set of exercises from Dr. Eric Chudler's site at the University of Washington; check out the demonstrations of blind spots, negative after-images, dark adaptation...lots more!

Mapping Receptive Fields: *http://www.psych.purdue.edu/~coglab/ReceptiveField/RF.html*

    From the Cognitive Psychology group at Purdue University, a nice exercise in determining the receptive fields of neurons in the visual system.

Color Vision: *http://www.hhmi.org/senses/b/b140.htm#"top"*

    From the Howard Hughes Medical Institute's *Hearing, Seeing and Smelling* site, a very good review..

Animation of Receptive Fields: *http://psychlab1.hanover.edu/Classes/Neuro/Internet/Receptive Fields/*

    From Dr. John Krantz at Hanover College, an animation illustrating the receptive fields of the retina. For animations of edge detectors, see:
        http://psychlab1.hanover.edu/Classes/Neuro/Internet/ReceptiveEdges

    NOTE: To view this, you need the PowerPoint animation player, available at:

        http://officeupdate.microsoft.com/features/AstPowerPoint.htm

Lecture 8a

CORTICAL MECHANISMS OF VISION AND AUDITION

Outline

1. Introductory Concepts
   a. The Traditional Hierarchical Sensory-System Model
   b. Sensation and Perception
   c. Hierarchical Organization

2. Cortical Mechanisms of Vision
   a. Scotomas and Blindsight
   b. Completion
   c. Secondary Visual Cortex and Association Cortex
   d. Visual Agnosia

3. Auditory System
   a. The Ear
   b. Auditory Projections
   c. Auditory Cortex
   d. Sound Localization

Lecture Notes

1. **Introductory Concepts**
   - we have discussed the visual system from the eye to the striate (primary visual) cortex
   - this lecture will focus on cortical mechanisms involved in the processing of sensory, visual, and auditory information

   a. **The Traditional Hierarchical Sensory-System Model**
      - it has been usual to think of sensory-system organization according to the following model; input flows from receptors to thalamus, to primary sensory cortex, to secondary sensory cortex, and finally to association cortex
      - **primary sensory cortex** is cortex that receives input directly from **thalamic sensory relay nuclei**; the **secondary sensory cortex** of a sensory system receives input primarily from the primary sensory cortex of that system; **association cortex** is cortex that receives input from more than one sensory system
      - the major feature of the traditional sensory-system model is its serial and hierarchical organization; a **hierarchical system** is any system with components that can be assigned to ranks
      - sensory systems are thought to be hierarchical in two ways: (1) sensory information is thought to flow through brain structures in order of their increasing neuroanatomical complexity, and (2) sensation is thought to be less complex than perception
      - the neuroanatomical hierarchy is thought to be related to the functional hierarchy; perception is often assumed to be a function of cortical structures

   b. **Sensation and Perception**
      - **sensation** refers to the simple process of detecting the presence of a stimulus; **perception** refers to the complex process of integrating, recognizing, and interpreting complex patterns of sensations
      - the need for this distinction is illustrated by the case of Dr. P, the man who mistook his wife for a hat; he had severe visual perception problems in the absence of disturbances of visual sensation

c. **The Current Parallel, Functionally Segregated Hierarchical Model of Sensory-System Organization**
    (use Digital Image Archive Figure CH08F02.BMP)
    - it is now clear that sensory systems are characterized by a parallel, functionally segregated, hierarchical organization:

    Parallel: sensory systems are organized so that information flows between different structures simultaneously along multiple pathways
    Functionally Segregated: sensory systems are organized so that different parts of the various structures specialize in different kinds of analysis.
    Hierarchical: as noted, information flows through brain structures in order of their increasing neuroanatomical and functional complexity.

    The Critical Question: If different types of information are processed in different specialized zones that are found in different structures connected by multiple pathways, how are complex stimuli perceived as an integrated whole? This is known as the **binding problem.**

2. **Cortical Mechanisms of Vision** *(use Digital Image Archive Figure CH08F03.BMP)*

    a. **Scotomas and Blindsight**
        - individuals with damage to primary visual cortex have **scotomas** or areas of blindness in the corresponding areas of the visual field; scotomas are plotted by **perimetry**
        - amazingly, when forced to guess, some brain-damaged patients can respond to stimuli in their scotomas (e.g., can grab a moving object or guess the direction of its movement), all the while claiming to see nothing; this is called **blindsight**
        - blindsight is thought to be mediated by visual pathways that are not part of the retina-geniculate-striate system; for example, one hypothesis is that the retina-geniculate-striate system mediates pattern and color perception, whereas a system involving the **superior colliculus** and the **pulvinar nucleus** of the thalamus mediates the detection and localization of objects in space
        - this phenomenon emphasizes that **parallel models** (multiple-path models), rather than **serial models** (single-path models), are needed to explain many perceptual phenomena

    b. **Completion**
        - many patients with large scotomas are unaware of them; for example, patients with the complete destruction of the left striate cortex cannot detect stimuli in their right visual fields (they are **hemianopic**), yet when they stare at a face, or even half a face that falls entirely in their left visual field, they report seeing an entire face; this phenomenon is called **completion**
        - use *Digital Image Archive Figure CH08F05.BMP* to describe Lashley's completion of his own migraine-related scotoma

    c. **Secondary Visual Cortex and Association Cortices** *(use Digital Image Archive Figure CH08F09.BMP)*
        - visual information is believed to flow along two anatomically and functionally distinct pathways:

        1) a **dorsal stream**, with information flowing from primary visual cortex through the dorsal prestriate secondary visual cortex to association cortex in the posterior parietal region; and
        2) a **ventral stream**, with information flowing from primary visual cortex through the dorsal prestriate secondary visual cortex to association cortex in the posterior parietal region.

        - traditionally, the dorsal stream was believed to be involved in the perception of where object are (a **where** system), while the ventral stream was believed to be involved in the recognition of that object (a **what** system).
        - more recently, Milner & Goodale (1993) have proposed that the dorsal stream is actually involved in directing behavioral interactions with objects (which would include, but not be restricted to, analyses of where objects are; a **behavioral control** path), while the ventral stream is responsible for the conscious recognition of objects (a **conscious perception** path).

d. **Visual Agnosia**
- **agnosia** is a failure to recognize that is not attributable to a simple sensory deficit, or to motor, verbal, or intellectual impairment (gnosis means "to know"); the case of Dr. P., the man who mistook his wife for a hat, is a classic example of **visual agnosia**
- **prosopagnosia**, the inability to recognize faces, is the most interesting and most common form of visual agnosia; prosopagnosics can readily recognize objects (chairs, tables, hats), but they have extreme difficulty telling one face from another; a prosopagnosic may even fail to recognize her or his own face in a mirror
- Tranel and Damasio (1985) showed that despite a lack of conscious recognition for familiar faces, prosopagnosics show skin conductance changes indicating a recognition of the faces at subconscious levels
- the existence of prosopagnosia has led to the view that there is a special area in the brain for the recognition of faces and that it is damaged in prosopagnosics; the finding of neurons in the inferotemporal cortices of monkeys and sheep that appear to respond only to conspecific faces supports this view *(use Digital Image Archive Figure CH08F010.BMP)*
- however, reports that a bird watcher and a farmer who suffered from prosopagnosia also lost their ability to recognize specific species of birds and specific cows, respectively, suggests that prosopagnosia may not be specific to faces; prosopagnosics may have difficulty distinguishing between visually similar members of complex classes of visual stimuli, of which faces are simply the most obvious class

3. **Auditory System**

a. **The Ear** *(use Digital Image Archive Figure CH08F13.BMP)*
- vibrations in the air are transmitted through the **tympanic membrane** (ear drum), **ossicles** (three small bones), and **oval window** into the fluid of the cochlea
- the vibrations bend the **organ of Corti** and excite **hair cells** in the **basilar membrane**
- the organization of the organ of Corti is **tonotopic**; higher frequencies excite receptors closer to the oval **window**, thus with exposure to noise as well as decrements due to age, damage to the high frequency receptors occurs first

b. **Auditory Projections** *(use Digital Image Archive Figure CH08F14.BMP)*
- unlike the visual system, there is no one major auditory projection
- **hair cells** synapse on neurons whose axons enter the **metencephalon** and synapse in the **cochlear nucleus**
- from the cochlear nucleus some fibers project to the nearby lateral and medial **superior olives**, and fibers from all three metencephalic nuclei ascend via the **lateral lemniscus** to the **inferiorcolliculus** of the mesencephalon
- from the inferior colliculus, fibers ascend to the **medial geniculate nucleus** of the thalamus; and from there, fibers ascend to the primary auditory cortex in the lateral fissure
- the projections from each ear are bilateral

c. **Auditory Cortex** *(use Digital Image Archive Figure CH08F15.BMP)*
- research showed that the auditory cortex of each cat under study was strictly **tonotopically** organized but that the tonotopic maps were different in different cats--this illustrates the danger of averaging
- anterior portions of auditory cortex tend to respond to higher frequencies and posterior portions to lower frequencies
- there are several different complete tonotopic cortical maps in each cat, but the significance of these different maps is not understood
- bilateral lesions of auditory cortex do not permanently eliminate the ability to hear, even if the lesions include secondary auditory cortex
- humans with extensive auditory cortex damage often have difficulty: (1) perceiving very brief stimuli, (2) discriminating among several sounds presented in rapid succession, (3) discriminating among different rapid sequences of sound, and (4) localizing sounds; thus they often have difficulty understanding speech; this is called **word deafness**, which is often the final stage in recovery from a more global dysfunction

d. **Sound Localization**
  - the superior olives play a role in sound localization; the **medial superior olives** contain neurons that are sensitive to differences in the time of arrival of a sound at the two ears; the **lateral superior olives** contain neurons that are sensitive to differences in the amplitude of a sound at the two ears; the layers of the **superior colliculus** that receive input from the superior olives are topographically organized
  - much of the research on sound localization has focused on the **barn owl** because of its amazing ability to locate mice in the dark; its **facial ruff** gives it the ability to locate sounds in the vertical dimension, an ability that most animals lack; because of the ruff, the barn owl's right ear is more sensitive to "high" sounds, and the left ear is more sensitive to "low" sounds; this effect is greater for higher frequencies; the barn owl's auditory system compares the intensities detected at each ear for each frequency in a sound in order to locate it; that is why they cannot locate single-frequency sounds in vertical space.

Suggested Websites for Lecture 8a:

What We Can Learn About Brain Function from Sensory Illusions: *http://www.hhmi.org/senses/a/a110.htm*

From the Howard Hughes Medical Institute's *Our Precious Senses* site, an interesting look at sensory illusions and what they reveal about the organization and function of our sensory systems. Many interesting figures and diagrams.

Audition: Cochlea: *http://www.hhmi.org/senses/c/c110.htm*

From the Howard Hughes Medical Institute's *Our Precious Senses* site, a good overview of the function of the hair cells in the cochlea and the transduction of sound energy into neural signals.

Central Visual Pathways: *http://thalamus.wustl.edu/course/cenvis.html*

From the Washington University School of Medicine, information about the organization of the visual system from the retina to higher-order visual cortex; includes information on the thalamus, primary visual cortex and ocular dominance columns, and the M- and P-pathways for visual information.

The Virtual Ear: *http://ctl.augie.edu/perry/ear/hearmech.htm*

From Perry Hanavan at Augustana College, a great collection of links to sites related to all parts of the auditory system, from the ear to auditory cortex.

Lecture 8b

**THE SOMATOSENSORY SYSTEM, THE CHEMICAL SENSES, AND
A GENERAL MODEL OF SENSORY SYSTEM ORGANIZATION**

Outline

1. Organization of the Somatosensory System
   a. The Somatosensory Subsystems
   b. Cutaneous Receptors
   c. The Two Ascending Pathways

2. Somatosensory Cortex

3. Pain and the Descending Analgesia Circuit

4. Smell and Taste
   a. The Olfactory System
   b. The Gustatory System

5. Selective Attention

6. Review of Current Models of Parallel, Functionally Segregated, Hierarchical Sensory Systems

Lecture Notes

1. Organization of the Somatosensory System

a. Somatosensation and the Somatosensory Subsystems
   - the somatosensory system comprises three subsystems: (1) an **exteroceptive** cutaneous system, (2) a **proprioception** system (monitors body position), and (3) an **interoceptive** system (monitors conditions within the body such as blood pressure)
   - we are going to focus on the exteroceptive cutaneous subsystem, which in turn comprises three somewhat distinct subsystems, which respond to: (1) mechanical stimulation of the skin (that is to **touch**), (2) thermal stimulation (temperature), and (3) nociceptive stimuli (surface pain)

b. Cutaneous Receptors and Dermatomes *(use Digital Image Archive Figure CH08F17.BMP)*
   - there are seven kinds of cutaneous receptors (see Figure 8.16 of BIOPSYCHOLOGY); for example there are (1) **free nerve endings**, which provide signals about pain and temperature; (2) **Pacinian corpuscles** which are deep fast-adapting touch receptors; (3) **Merkel receptors,** and (4) **Ruffini corpuscles,** which are slow-adapting touch receptors
   - the axons carrying sensory information from cutaneous receptors gather together in nerves and enter the spinal cord via the **dorsal roots** *(use Digital Image Archive Figure CH03F19.BMP)*
   - the area of the body that is innervated by the left and right dorsal roots of a given segment of the spinal cord is called a **dermatome** ("skin slice"; *use Digital Image Archive Figure CH08F18.BMP);* **overlap between adjacent dermatomes means that destruction of a single dorsal root does not produce complete somatosensory loss**

c.   The Two Ascending Pathways

1) **The Dorsal-Column Medial-Lemniscus System**: *(use Digital Image Archive Figure CH08F19.BMP)*

- the dorsal-column medial-lemniscus system carries information about **touch** and **proprioception** to the cortex; the axons of receptors in the skin enter the spinal cord and ascend in the ipsilateral dorsal columns to the **dorsal column nuclei**, the axons of dorsal-column-nuclei cells decussate and ascend in the **medial lemniscus** to the **ventral posterior nucleus** (VPN); the axons of VPN cells ascend to the somatosensory cortex
- axons from the toes that ascend in the dorsal columns are the longest in the body

2) **The Anterolateral System**: : *(use Digital Image Archive Figure CH08F20.BMP)*

- the other ascending somatosensory pathway
- the anterolateral system carries some crude information about touch, but its primary function is to mediate the perception of **pain** and **temperature**
- axons in the anterolateral system synapse as soon as they enter the cord; the second-order axons **decussate immediately** and ascend in one of three different anterolateral pathways:
  (1) the **spinothalamic tract**, which projects to the ventral posterior nucleus of the thalamus;
        (2) the **spinoreticular tract**, which projects to the reticular formation and then to the **parafascicular** and **intralaminar nuclei of the thalamus**; and
            (3) the **spinotectal tract,** which projects to the mesencephalic **tectum**
- Mark and his colleagues found that lesions to the VP thalamus produce a loss of somatosensation and sharp pain perception, while lesions to the parafascicular and intralaminar nuclei of the thalamus reduced perception of chronic pain without disrupting cutaneous sensitivity.

2.   **Somatosensory Cortex:** *(use Digital Image Archive Figure CH08F21.BMP)*

- the various thalamic nuclei receiving somatosensory information project to: (1) primary somatosensory cortex (**SI**) in the **postcentral gyrus**, (2) secondary somatosensory cortex (**SII**), which is ventral to SI, and (3) to the **posterior parietal cortex**
- the primary somatosensory cortex is organized somatotopically; it is known as the **somatosensory homunculus**; studies by Kaas, Nelson, Sur, & Merzenich (1981) have shown that instead of one homunculus (as indicated by the classic early studies of Penfield), primary somatosensory cortex comprises **four parallel somatotopically organized strips**, each sensitive to a different kind of somatosensory input
- cortical lesions to primary somatosensory cortex have only minor effects on tactual sensitivity--mainly on the sensitivity of the hands
- large lesions to parietal cortex occasionally produce **somatosensory agnosias**; for example (1) **astereognosia**, the loss of the ability to recognize objects by touch in the absence of defects in somatosensation (**stereognosis** is the ability to identify an object by touch); and (2) **asomatognosia**, loss of the ability to recognize parts of one's own body (e.g., the case of Aunt Betty; described in chapter 8 of BIOPSYCHOLOGY)

3.   **Pain and the Descending Analgesia Circuit**

- although most people think of pain as bad, it is very adaptive; cases of **congenital pain insensitivity** rarely survive their teens (e.g., they suffer many burns, lacerations, and joint problems, and any internal disorder such as appendicitis is lethal (see the case of Miss C. in Chapter 8 of BIOPSYCHOLOGY)
- in contrast to what most people believe, the severity of pain is poorly related to the amount of damage; for example, athletes are often unaware of severe injuries until after the game
- recently PET has been used to study cortical localization of pain; only the **anterior cingulate cortex** has been consistently implicated in cortical perception of pain; however it appears that this activation is more related to **emotional responses** to pain rather than the perception of pain

- Melzack and Wall (1965) were impressed by the ability of emotional and cognitive factors to block pain; they concluded that there must be a circuit descending from the forebrain that can block incoming pain signals (gate-control theory)
- the first direct evidence of such a descending analgesia circuit came from the discovery that stimulation of the **periaqueductal gray** (PAG) produced analgesia in rats; surgery could be performed under PAG-stimulation-produced analgesia
- next, it was discovered that there were receptors for opiate analgesics (e.g., morphine) in the PAG and several other sites; this suggested that the body produced its own opiates (called endogenous opiates or **endorphins**), and several were subsequently isolated
- several lines of evidence led Basbaum and Fields to propose a **descending analgesia circuit** (*use Digital Image Archive Figure CH08F21.BMP*); the circuit goes from the PAG to the **raphé nucleus** and then descends via the dorsal columns to the dorsal horns of the spinal cord
- the following are three of the pieces of evidence that support Basbaum and Field's model: (1) microinjection of opiate antagonists, such as naloxone, into the PAG blocks the analgesia produced by systemic injection of morphine, (2) electrical stimulation of the raphé inhibits pain signals entering the spinal cord, (3) lesioning the raphé or dorsal columns blocks the analgesia produced by PAG stimulation
- one of the most interesting pain phenomena is **phantom limb pain**; it is chronic severe pain that is experienced by about 50% of amputees; paradoxically, surgical treatments have proven ineffective

4. Smell and Taste

a. The Olfactory System (*use Digital Image Archive Figure CH08F25.BMP*)
- smell is an olfactory system response to airborne chemicals
- many animals respond to **pheromones,** smells released by an animal to influence the behavior of conspecifics
- chemical stimuli are processed as follows: (1) transduction of olfactory stimuli occurs in olfactory receptors located in the **olfactory mucosa** of the upper nasal cavity; (2) these cells send their axons through the **cribriform plate** to synapse on cells in the **olfactory bulbs**; (3) these neurons then send axons directly to the **pyriform cortex** and **amygdala** of the temporal lobes (making olfaction the one sensory modality that gains access to the telencephalon without passing through the thalamus); (4) these areas project to to various parts of the **limbic system** (which is responsible for the emotional perception of odorants) and to the **medial dorsal nucleus of the thalamus**; and (5) the dorsomedial nucleus of the thalamus eventually passes the olfactory information on to the **orbitofrontal cortex** where the odor is consciously perceived.
- **anosmia** is an inability to smell; commonly caused by damage to the olfactory nerves passing through the cribriform plate.
- **ageusia** is an inability to taste; it is rare, but may be caused by damage to the facial nerve.

b. The Gustatory System (*use Digital Image Archive Figure CH08F27.BMP*)
- taste operates in tandem with smell; gustatory receptors are called **taste buds**
- there are 4 primary tastes: **sweet, sour, bitter** and **salty**; however, these perceptions do not match up nicely with 4 simple gustatory receptors
- gustatory stimuli are processed as follows: (1) gustatory stimuli are transduced by taste buds on the tongue and oral cavity; (2) axons from these receptors projects via the facial nerves (CN VII), the glossopharyngeal nerves (CN IX), and the vagus nerves (CN X) to the **solitary nucleus** of the medulla; which projects to (4) the **ventral posterior nucleus** of the thalamus; neurons there relay the gustatory information to (5) **primary gustatory cortex** (near the facial region of SI) and **secondary gustatory cortex** (found deep in the lateral fissure).

5. Selective Attention
- allows us to **consciously perceive** just a fraction of what we **unconsciously sense**
- may be **top-down** or **bottom-up**
- has been demonstrated behaviorally as well as on the effects of sensory stimuli on the spike activity of single neurons

- **change blindness** is classic example of the effects of selective attention; so is the **cocktail phenomenon**

6. Review of Current General Models of Parallel, Functionally Segregated, Hierarchical Sensory Systems
   - (*use Digital Image Archive Figure CH08F02.BMP*)
   - this model emphasizes four aspects of sensory-system organization: (1) sensory systems are **hierarchical,** (2) sensory systems are **parallel,** (3) sensory systems project to the cortex via the **thalamus** (except for olfaction); 4) there are **multiple representations** of each sensory system in the cortex
   - research has revealed two other general principles of sensory-system organization: (5) sensory cortex is often **topographically organized** in a systematic fashion, and (6) sensory cortex is organized in columns

Suggested Websites for Lecture 8b:

Supertasters and Taste Intensity: *http://www.sfn.org/briefings/taste.html*

From the Society for Neuroscience's *Brain Briefings*, an overview of the tastebuds of the tongue and why some people have better....taste? See also:

http://ificinfo.health.org/insight/exper.htm

for more information about this gustatory sense

Pain: Controlling Cancer's Pain: http://www.sciam.com/0996issue/0996foley.html

From Scientific American, a good article on modern approaches to pain control. See also:

http://www.sciam.com/explorations/0492melzak.html

for an interesting article by Dr. Ronald Melzack on the phenomenon of phantom limbs.

The Somatosensory System: Body: *http://thalamus.wustl.edu/course/bassens.html*

From the Washington University School of Medicine, a wonderful page devoted to the organization and function of the somatosensory system, including the pain and proprioceptive systems.

The Organs of Smell: *http://www.hhmi.org/senses/d/d110.htm*

Text and figures about the neural bases of smell, from the Howard Hughes Medical Institute. A very good figure of the olfactory pathways in the brain, and information about the vomeronasal organ and the "accessory" olfactory system.

Lecture 9a

FOREBRAIN STRUCTURES OF THE SENSORIMOTOR SYSTEM

Outline

1. Principles of Sensorimotor Function
   a. Hierarchical Organization
   b. Motor Output is Guided by Sensory Input
   c. Learning Changes the Locus of Sensorimotor Control

2. Posterior Parietal Association Cortex
   a. Apraxia
   b. Contralateral Neglect
   c. Astereognosia

3. Dorsolateral Prefrontal Association Cortex

4. Secondary Motor Cortex
   a. Premotor Cortex
   b. Supplementary Motor Area
   c. Cingulate Motor Areas

5. Primary Motor Cortex

6. Cerebellum and Basal Ganglia
   a. Cerebellum
   b. Basal Ganglia

Lecture Notes

1. **Principles of Sensorimotor Function** *(use Digital Image Archive Figure CH09F01.BMP)*

   a. **Hierarchical Organization**
      - the sensorimotor system is organized like a large effective company; the president issues general commands and lower levels take care of details; the advantage of this hierarchical arrangement is that higher levels are left free to focus on complex functions

   b. **Motor Output is Guided by Sensory Input**
      - like a large company, the sensorimotor system carefully monitors the external world and the consequences of its own actions, and it acts accordingly; only **ballistic movements** are not guided by sensory feedback
      - note the case of G.O., a former darts champion who suffered an infection that destroyed the somatosensory nerves of his arms; even though he still had visual feedback, he had difficulty picking up buttons or coins, difficulty adjusting to unanticipated external forces, and difficulty maintaining a constant force (e.g., holding a pen, cup, or suitcase)

   c. **Learning Changes the Locus of Sensorimotor Control**
      - as a new company develops, more and more tasks become part of the routine and are taken over by lower levels of the organization; the same thing happens in the sensorimotor system; after much practice lower levels perform well-learned tasks with little higher involvement

- think of some of the skills that you have learned (e.g., typing, skiing, piano playing)
- Why is the sensorimotor system like a large company in these three important respects? Is it mere coincidence? No, they are both complex behavioral systems that have evolved under the pressure to survive in competitive environments; thus it is not surprising that efficient companies and sensorimotor systems have a lot in common

2. **Posterior Parietal Association Cortex** *(use Digital Image Archive Figure CH09F02.BMP)*

- before an effective response can be initiated, the sensorimotor system must know the positions of various parts of the body and of objects in the external world; current thinking is that the **posterior parietal cortex** performs this function
- the posterior parietal cortex receives input from visual, auditory, and somatosensory systems (that is why it is considered to be association cortex); most of its output goes to secondary motor cortex
- in addition to disrupting the accuracy of movements, large lesions of posterior cortex can produce **apraxia** and **contralateral neglect**

a. **Apraxia**
- apraxia is the inability to perform movements when requested to do so (in the absence of simple sensory or motor deficits, motivational deficits, or intellectual deficits); for example, an apraxic patient may have difficulty demonstrating hammering movements when asked to do so (even when they are demonstrated to him or her) but be perfectly capable of spontaneously hammering a nail
- apraxia is almost always associated with left hemisphere damage, but its symptoms are always bilateral
- right parietal damage often produces deficits on the **WAIS block-design subtest**; this is referred to as **constructional apraxia**

b. **Contralateral Neglect**
- patients with contralateral neglect fail to respond to visual, auditory, or somatosensory stimuli from the contralateral half of the body
- contralateral neglect is usually produced by very large right parietal lesions
- patients with contralateral neglect may shave only the right half of their face, eat food from only the right half of their plate, or put only their right leg in their pants; for example, the case of Mrs. S. in chapter 9 of BIOPSYCHOLOGY

3. **Dorsolateral Prefrontal Association Cortex** *(use Digital Image Archive Figure CH09F04.BMP)*

- projections to this area are received from the posterior parietal cortex; this area in turn projects to parts of the **secondary motor cortex**, the **primary cortex**, and to the **frontal eye field**
- based on experiments using primates, it has been suggested that one function of the prefrontal association cortex is to provide a **mental representation** of stimuli to which the subject will respond
- further research shows that the motor neurons firing the earliest (prior to a motor task) are located in the dorsolateral prefrontal cortex, indicating that this area may be key in decisions regarding **voluntary response initiation**
- the sensory information supplied by the posterior parietal association cortex would allow a basis for such decision making

4. **Secondary Motor Cortex** *(use Digital Image Archive Figure CH09F05.BMP)*

- there are three areas of secondary motor cortex: the **premotor cortex**, the **supplementary motor area**, and the **cingulate motor areas.** They all send information to primary motor cortex; all receive input from primary motor cortex; all are interconnected with one another; and all send axons to the motor circuits of the brainstem

a. Premotor Cortex
- unlike the supplementary motor area, the primary input to the premotor cortex is **visual;** like the supplementary motor area, the premotor cortex is involved in preparation for movement and in **externally guided movements** that are iniated and guided by external cues.

b. Supplementary Motor Area
- much of the supplementary motor area (SMA) is in the **longitudinal fissure**; SMA stimulation produces complex patterned movements rather than individual muscle contractions; many supplementary motor cortex neurons tend to become active just before a voluntary response
- unlike the premotor cortex, the major input to the supplementary motor area is from the **somatosensory cortex;** the supplementary motor area is particularly important to learning new motor sequences
- believed to have key role in generation of **self-generated movements** that are guided by internal representations of the stimuli

c. Cingulate Motor Areas
- lie on the cingulate gyrus, just below the SMA
- specific function not clear

5. Primary Motor Cortex *(use Digital Image Archive Figure CH09F07.BMP)*

- **primary motor cortex** is in the precentral gyrus of the frontal lobe; it is somatotopically organized; its organization was discovered by Penfield, who stimulated the cortices of conscious patients during brain surgery
- the **motor homunculus** has a disproportionate representation of hands and mouth; in fact, two different areas of each primary motor cortex control the contralateral hand
- each area of primary motor cortex receives feedback from the muscles and joints that it influences; one of the hand areas receives input from the skin; this feedback is presumably important for **stereognosis**
- lesions of primary motor cortex produce contralateral **astereognosia**; they reduce the speed and force of contralateral movements, and they make it difficult to move one body part (e.g., a finger) independently of others. THEY DO NOT PRODUCE PARALYSIS…

6. Cerebellum and Basal Ganglia

- the cerebellum and basal ganglia are both important subcortical sensorimotor structures, but neither participates directly in the transmission of signals to the spinal cord
- their role seems to be to **integrate and coordinate** the activity of structures at various levels of the sensorimotor system

a. Cerebellum *(use Digital Image Archive Figure CH03F23.BMP) AND Figure CH03F31.BMP)*
- the cerebellum (means little brain) constitutes only 10% of the brain's mass, but it contains over half the brain's neurons; it is organized systematically in **lobes**
- it is thought to receive signals about plans of action from the premotor cortex, about descending signals from brain stem nuclei, and feedback from somatosensory and **vestibular** systems
- it is thought to **correct deviations** from intended movements
- effects of diffuse cerebellar damage include loss of the ability to precisely control movement, to adjust motor output to changing conditions, to maintain steady postures, exhibit good locomotion, to maintain balance, to speak clearly etc.
- long-recognized role in **motor learning**, and more recently appreciated for a role in learning of **nonmotor cognitive responses**

b. Basal Ganglia *(use Digital Image Archive Figure CH03F31.BMP)*
- the basal ganglia are part of a loop that receives information from various parts of the cortex and transmits it back to motor cortices via the thalamus
- basal ganglia are involved in selection and initiation of motor sequences, in motor learning, and in learning of nonmotor cognitive tasks.
- basal ganglia function compromised in patients with **Parkinson's Disease** (due to loss of dopamine from substantia nigra) and **Huntington's Disease** (due to loss of cells in basal ganglia)

Suggested Websites for Lecture 9a:

The Basic Motor Pathway: *http://thalamus.wustl.edu/course/basmot.html*

From the Washington University School of Medicine, a good text-n-figure description of the corticospinal pathway from motor cortex to the spinal cord.

Basal Ganglia and Cerebellum: *http://thalamus.wustl.edu/course/cerebell.html*

A very good text-and-figure site from Washington University's School of Medicine, explaining the anatomy and function of the basal ganglia and the cerebellum. Excellent; includes circuit drawings; histological images; well-written.

Gross Anatomy of CNS Motor System: *http://www9.biostr.washington.edu/da.html*

From the Interactive Brain Atlas from the Digital Anatomist Project at the University of Washington, some good illustrations of the central motor pathways. From this page, select Interactive Brain Atlas, then either 3-D Objects, 3-D Object Composites, or 3-D Pathways for images of the basal ganglia, the cerebellum, and the corticospinal pathways.

Motor Cortex and Movement: *http://www.sciam.com/0696issue/0696techbus02.html*

An interesting article from Scientific American on what single-unit recordings in primate motor cortex reveal about the neural bases of movement.

Lecture 9b

SPINAL SENSORIMOTOR PATHWAYS AND CIRCUITS

Outline

1. Descending Motor Pathways

2. Sensorimotor Spinal Circuits
   a. Muscles
   b. Muscle Receptor Organs
   c. Reciprocal Innervation
   d. Recurrent Collateral Inhibition

3. Reflexes
   a. Withdrawal Reflex
   b. Stretch Reflex

4. Central Sensorimotor Programs

Lecture Notes

- we have already examined the cortical areas involved in the control of movement; today I will describe the pathways that descend from the primary motor cortex to the spinal sensorimotor circuits

1. Descending Motor Pathways

- there are four descending motor pathways on each side of the spinal cord; two descend in the dorsolateral areas of the spinal cord: (1) the **dorsolateral corticospinal tract** and (2) the **dorsolateral corticorubrospinal tract**; and two descend in the ventromedial areas of the spinal cord: (3) the **ventromedial corticospinal tract** and (4) the **ventromedial cortico-brainstem-spinal tract**

1) The Dorsolateral Motor Tracts *(use Digital Image Archive Figure CH09F09.BMP)*
- most axons in the dorsolateral corticospinal tract and all of those in the dorsolateral corticorubrospinal tract synapse on interneuron pools in the **contralateral spinal gray matter** that control motor neurons of distal limb muscles
- however, in primates and some other mammalian species, **Betz cells** in the primary motor cortex descend contralaterally in the dorsolateral corticospinal tract and synapse on **motor neurons** that control the large weight-bearing muscles of the legs
- also primates and a few other mammals capable of individual digit movement have dorsolateral corticospinal tract neurons that synapse directly on motor neurons

2) The Ventromedial Tracts *(use Digital Image Archive Figure CH09F10.BMP)*
- the axons of the ventromedial corticospinal tract **descend ipsilaterally** and **terminate bilaterally** in several segments of the spinal cord on the interneuron pools that control the motor neurons of trunk and proximal limb muscles on both sides of the body; the information delivery is more diffuse and goes to more levels than via dorsolateral paths
- the axons of the ventromedial cortico-brainstem-spinal tract also descend and terminate diffusely on the interneuron pools influencing trunk and proximal limb muscles on both sides of the body

- the different functions of these four tracts are demonstrated by the experiment of Lawrence and Kuypers (1968) on monkeys:

    - first, they cut the dorsolateral corticospinal tracts at the **medullary pyramids**; the monkeys lost their ability to move individual fingers and to release objects in their grasp (revealing the role of the dorsolateral corticospinal pathway in **individual or fine movements** of the digits); however, they had no difficulty releasing bars and branches when they were climbing
    - next all of the monkeys received a second operation.

        a) Half of the monkeys received a dorsolateral corticorubrospinal tract transection; these monkeys could stand, walk, and climb normally; but when they sat, their arms hung limply by their sides, and they were used like rubber-handled rakes. Thus, the corticorubrospinal tract seems to control the **reaching movements of the limbs.**

        b) The other half of the monkeys received a transection of both ventromedial tracts (only their dorsolateral corticorubrospinal tract remained intact); these monkeys had great difficulty walking or even sitting (a noise would make them fall over); when they fed, they did so with elbow and whole-hand movements. Thus, the ventromedial paths seem to be involved with **whole-body movements and postural control.**

2. **Sensorimotor Spinal Circuits**

    a. **Muscles**
        - review the anatomy of the motor end-plate, the neuromuscular junction, and the role of acetylcholine
        - **motor units** include a single motor neuron and all of the muscle fibers that it innervates; motor unit size is dependent on the movement accuracy required
        - **motor pools** include all motor neurons that innervate fibers of a single muscle
        - **flexors** (bend or flex a joint) vs. **extensors** (straighten or extend a limb)
        - **synergistic** (muscles that produce the same type of movement, either flexion or extension, at a joint) vs. **antagonistic** (muscles whose actions oppose one another at a joint)
        - **dynamic contraction** (one where muscles shorten to produce action at a joint) vs. **isometric contraction** (one where muscle tension increases, but muscle does not shorten and there is not actin at joint)

    b. **Muscle Receptor Organs** *(use Digital Image Archive Figure CH09F14.BMP)*
        - **Golgi tendon organs** are embedded in tendons; **muscle spindles** are embedded in muscles
        - because Golgi tendon organs are connected in **series** with muscles, they are sensitive to muscle tension; in contrast, muscle spindles are connected in **parallel** with the muscle fibers and they are sensitive to muscle length

    c. **Reciprocal Innervation** *(use Digital Image Archive Figure CH09F18.BMP)*
        - when a muscle contracts, antagonist muscles automatically relax; this is mediated by inhibitory interneurons
        - however, there is always some degree of **co-contraction**, for smoother, more precise movement

    d. **Recurrent Collateral Inhibition**
        - when a motor neuron fires, an axon collateral feeds onto an inhibitory interneuron in the ventral horn (i.e., onto a **Renshaw cell**), which synapses on the cell body of the motor neuron that activated it; thus motor neurons take an enforced rest after firing; this distributes the work load among the muscle's motor pool)

3. **Reflexes**

    a. **Withdrawal Reflex**
- sensory neurons carrying signals evoked by a painful stimulus to a hand or foot synapse on interneurons that synapse on flexors of the same limb
- thus, about 1.6 millisecond (the time for a signal to be transmitted across a two synapses) after the painful stimulus, a burst of action potentials can be recorded in the flexor motor nerves of the same limb, and the limb is withdrawn
- the limb is withdrawn before information about the painful event reaches the brain

    b. **Stretch Reflex** *(use Digital Image Archive Figure CH09F16.BMP)*
- you have all had your **patellar tendon reflex** tested by a doctor; the doctor raps the tendon of your relaxed thigh muscle, this stretches your thigh muscle and elicits an immediate compensatory contraction that makes your foot swing up; the patellar tendon reflex is a **stretch reflex**
- notice that this reflex is monosynaptic
- the function of the **intrafusal motor neuron** is to adjust the length of the intrafusal muscle in relation to extrafusal muscle length to maintain the muscle spindle's sensitivity to changes in extrafusal muscle length *(use Digital Image Archive Figure CH09F15.BMP)*
- the function of the muscle-spindle feedback circuit is to make automatic adjustments in muscle tension in response to external forces
- the brain sends general instructions to the motor neurons (e.g., hold the glass of water), and the muscle spindle feedback circuit automatically adjusts the activity in the motor neurons to make sure that this instruction is carried out even if there are unanticipated external influences (e.g., somebody brushing against the arm)

4. **Central Sensorimotor Programs**

- the withdrawal and stretch reflexes are relatively simple reflexes; most reflexes involve integrated changes in several circuits in different segments of the spinal cord in response to sensory information supplied from various parts of the body (particularly from the vestibular and proprioception systems); for example, regaining one's balance after stumbling or a falling cat's landing on four paws

- Grillner (1985) showed that coordinated walking movements occurred in cats whose brains had been separated from their spinal cord if the cats were held over a treadmill; this suggests that the programs for some complex motor activities are wired into the spinal cord; these **central sensorimotor programs** are analogous to the protocols for a procedural automation

- central sensorimotor programs appear to be organized in a hierarchical fashion, with lower programs carrying out general instructions received from higher programs. Once activated, the lower levels of the nervous system can act on the basis of sensory information without further involvement of the higher levels of the hierarchy.

- sensorimotor learning **"chunks"** central sensorimotor programs and transfers their control to lower levels of the CNS

- **practice** is not necessary for the development of some central sensorimotor programs (e.g., Fentress's work on grooming movements in mice); others require practice of the motor response for correct learning to occur.

Suggested Websites for Lecture 9b:

Spinal Mechanisms of Movement: *http://thalamus.wustl.edu/course/spinal.html*

See this site for a good description of the organization of motor pathways in the spinal cord, and of the spinal circuits involved in the deep-tendon (muscle stretch) reflex and the golgi tendon organ (GTO) reflex. See also:

http://www.ptd.neu.edu/neuroanatomy/cyberclass/spinalcontrol/

for another excellent source of information about spinal mechanisms of movement.

The Annotated Muscle Spindle: *http://www.umds.ac.uk/physiology/mcal/spin2.html*

From King's College, London, a very informative point'n'tell diagram describing the anatomy and basic function of the muscle spindle.

Myasthenia Gravis and Disorders of the Neuromuscular Junction:

http://www.neuro.wustl.edu/neuromuscular/index.html

From Washington University's School of Medicine, a great resource on neuromuscular disorders.

Animation of the Stretch Reflex:

http://psychlab1.hanover.edu/Classes/Neuro/Internet/Stretch%20Reflex/index.html

From John Krantz at Hanover College, an animation of the stretch reflex; requires the Powerpoint Animation viewer (which can be downloaded from this site).

Lecture 10a

THE DUAL-CENTER SET-POINT
MODEL OF EATING

Outline:

1. The Early Studies

2. Glucostatic and Lipostatic Theories v. Positive-Incentive Theories
    a. Glucostatic and Lipostatic Theories
    b. Positive-Incentive Theories

3. Hypothalamic Hunger and Satiety Centers and The Dual-Center Set-Point Model
    a. Ventromedial Hypothalamus
    b. Lateral Hypothalamus

4. Positive-Incentive Models of Feeding

5. Current Research on the Biopsychology of Eating
    a. Palatability and Positive Incentives
    b Energy Expenditure and Body-Fat Homeostasis
    c. Satiety Peptides
    d. Reevaluation of the Role of the Ventral Hypothalamus
    e. Role of Learning in Eating

6. A Settling-Point Model of Body-Weight Regulation

Lecture Notes

1. **The Early Studies** *(use Digital Image Archive Figure CH10F01.BMP)*

    -   energy is available in three forms (1) **lipids** (fats), (2) **proteins** (broken into amino acids), and (3) **glucose** (simple sugar byproducts of carbohydrates)
    -   energy metabolism occurs in three phases *(use Digital Image Archive Figure CH10F03.BMP)*; the **cephalic** phase (preparatory), **absorptive** phase (energy absorbed into the bloodstream), and the **fasting** phase (body utilizes food stores)
    -   the first influential study of the physiological basis of hunger was conducted in 1912 by **Canon and Washburn**; Washburn swallowed a balloon on the end of a thin tube, the balloon was partially inflated, and a pressure gauge was attached to the other end of the tube
    -   each time that he had a large stomach contraction, Washburn reported a pang of hunger; this led to the view that stomach contractions are a major factor in hunger.
    -   the finding that animals whose stomachs had been **denervated** or completely removed ate enough to maintain their body weights discredited this view; in addition, people with no stomachs report feeling hungry and maintain their body weights; they eat less per meal, but they eat more meals
    -   more recently, Koopman *(use Digital Image Archive Figure CH10F12.BMP)* has used a second-stomach preparation to implicate the gut in feeding behavior; rats who have had a second stomach implanted into their peritoneum eat less when the second stomach is loaded with food, even though the stomach is not innervated nor are the nutrients able to be absorbed into the bloodstream.

2. **Glucostatic and Lipostatic Theories**

   - research on feeding has been heavily influenced by the idea of a feeding **set-point,** based around the idea of a homeostatic, negative feedback system regulating feeding.
   - research on feeding has been strongly influenced by the idea that feeding is controlled by deviations from two different **set points:** a set point for **blood glucose (short-term regulation)** and a set point for **body fat (long-term regulation)**

3. **Hypothalamic Hunger and Satiety Centers and The Dual-Center Set-Point Model**

   - in the 1950's, studies in which various areas of the rat hypothalamus were lesioned or stimulated seemed to suggest that it contained the hypothesized **hunger** and **satiety centers**

   a. **Ventromedial Hypothalamus (VMH)** *(use Digital Image Archive Figure CH10F08.BMP)*
   - large bilateral lesions of the VMH produced hyperphagia and gross obesity; after the lesion, the rats were extremely hyperphagic and gained weight rapidly (**dynamic phase**); after several weeks hyperphagia was only slight and a new very high body weight was defended (**static phase**)
   - although several nuclei were damaged by the large VMH lesions, the syndrome was typically attributed to **ventromedial nucleus** damage
   - two interpretations were proposed: (1) that glucoreceptors and their associated satiety circuits had been destroyed, or (2) that the body-fat set point had been increased
   - electrical stimulation of the ventromedial nucleus caused hungry rats to stop eating; this finding is difficult to interpret due to the many reasons why electrical stimulation might have this effect (e.g., it might produce pain or nausea)

   b. **Lateral Hypothalamus (LH)** *(use Digital Image Archive Figure CH10F08.BMP)*
   - large bilateral lesions of the lateral hypothalamus rendered rats **aphagic** and **adipsic**; if force fed and then maintained on highly palatable wet diets, they eventually recovered to the point that they could maintain themselves on laboratory chow and water
   - lateral hypothalamic stimulation elicited feeding (and a variety of other motivated behaviors); the fact that satiated rats ran a maze to obtain food if they were stimulated, suggested that lateral hypothalamic stimulation induced hunger rather than mere eating movements
   - these data led to the development of a **dual-center, set-point model** of feeding behavior; this model reigned supreme in the 1950s and 1960s
   - the dual-center set-point model is based on two assumptions that have been rendered untenable by modern research: (1) that eating is normally a product of internal energy deficits; (2) that the homeostasis of the body's energy resources implies set-point regulation of eating

4. **Positive-Incentive Models of Feeding**

   - there are many problems with the theory that deviations from a blood-glucose or fat set point are the primary signals for hunger and satiety, and that the VMH and the LH are the satiety and hunger centers in the brain, respectively
   - for example, the idea of set-point controls for feeding are not evolutionarily sound; major predictions of the theories have not been supported by research in the area (e.g., people with **diabetes mellitus** overeat despite very high blood glucose levels; data indicate that VMH lesions seem to disrupt metabolism rather than feeding, and may be due to damage to structures in the region of the VMH like the **paraventricualr nucleus** of the hypothalamus, rather than the VMH itself
   - in addition, , they do not recognize the major influences of **taste, learning** and **social factors** on feeding.
   - recently, an alternative theory of feeding and hunger has emerged: the **positive-incentive theory**
   - this is based on the idea that we eat because eating is **pleasurable**, rather than to satisfy some setpoint for glucose or fat. When good food is present we will eat...regardless of whether we actually need the food or not. Hunger is determined by many factors including taste, previous experience with a food, time since your last meal, who you are eating with, etc.

5. Current Research on Biopsychology of Eating

- current research on the biopsychology of eating has seriously undermined the dual-center set-point theory and the assumptions on which it is based

a. Palatability and Positive Incentives
- the idea that eating is rigidly controlled by deviations from internal set points is humbled by a piece of pecan pie and whipped cream served at the end of a large meal; in rats, a small amount of saccharin added to their diet leads to an increase in consumption and marked weight gain
- such observations cannot be explained by the set-point theory; they have led to the idea that feeding is normally initiated by the **positive-incentive properties** of food (i.e., the anticipated pleasurable effects) rather than by internal deficits; the positive-incentive theory explains the effects of deprivation by assuming that deprivation increases a food's positive incentive properties--the anticipated pleasure from eating is assumed to be greater in individuals who have been deprived of food
- **sensory-specific satiety** also creastes problems; research suggests that eating a particular food reduces the incentive value of its taste more than that of other foods; thus if rats are offered a **cafeteria diet**, their consumption and weight increase dramatically; this is the kind of diet on which virtually all humans in industrialized societies currently exist; it is no wonder that obesity is a problem

b. Energy Expenditure and Body-Fat Homeostasis
- one problem with the dual-center set-point model is that it assumes that all regulation of the body's energy resources occurs on the intake side of the system; there is now strong evidence that the body responds to energy shortages and excesses by increasing or decreasing the efficiency of **energy utilization**
- as individuals gain weight, more and more of the calories that are consumed are wasted by excess heat production (**diet-induced thermogenesis**)
- with decreased amounts of stored fat, the body naturally slows its metabolic rate; this saves energy resources but makes further weight loss more difficult
- when more calories are consumed, the body no longer needs to conserve energy, thus metabolic rates increase and further weight gain becomes more difficult
- the interactions between energy resources of the body and the incentive properties of food have become important areas of research.

c. Satiety Peptides
- as noted earlier, several lines of recent research have suggested that food in the gastrointestinal tract causes the release of satiety signals
- for example, Koopman found that food injected into the stomach inhibits intake, even in vagotomized subjects and even when the food is not allowed to pass into the duodenum to be digested; perhaps this satiety signal is one of the many **peptide hormones** released from the gastrointestinal tract into the bloodstream
- **cholecystokinin** (CCK), **bombesin, glucagon**, and **somatostatin** injections have been shown to inhibit eating; recently, **neuropeptide Y** and **galanin** have been shown to increase feeding

d. Reevaluation of the Role of the Ventral Hypothalamus
- the hyperphagia and obesity produced by large bilateral VMH lesions was at first taken as evidence that the ventromedial nucleus is a satiety center; there are currently few adherents to this view
- the current view is that the VMH controls energy metabolism not satiety; VMH lesions have been shown to increase **lipogenesis** (production and storage of body fat) and decrease **lipolysis** (breakdown and use of body fat)
- paradoxically, it seems that rats with VMH lesions overeat because they are getting fat and not vice versa; in VMH-lesioned rats, glucose is continuously drawn from the blood and stored as fat, thus the rats must eat continually to supply themselves with a source of immediate energy

- the following four observations support this view:

    (1) **hyperinsulinemia** is observed after VMH-lesions, even in rats not allowed to eat, and the degree of hyperinsulinemia in a particular animal predicts its subsequent weight gain;
    (2) rats with VMH lesions gain more weight than controls, even when they are not allowed to eat more than controls;
    (3) during the day, when they sleep, rats with VMH lesions get their energy from **gluconeogenesis**; and
    (4) cutting the branch of the <u>vagus</u> nerve that conducts signals from the hypothalamus to the **pancreas** eliminates the hyperinsulemia and the hyperphagia produced by VMH lesions

- evidence indicates that many aspects of the VMH do not result from damage to the ventromedial nuclei per se; VMH lesions inevitably damage fibers coursing by the VMN on their way to the **paraventricular nuclei** *(use Digital Image Archive Figure CH10F010.BMP)*; hyperphagia, obesity, and hyperinsulemia are produced by discrete bilateral knife cuts to these passing fibers or to lesions of the paraventricular nuclei themselves

e. **Role of Learning in Eating**
   - recent research has shown that learning can influence eating in a variety of ways
   - in general animals are born with a preference for sweet and salty tastes and with an aversion to bitter tastes; but they learn to avoid any taste followed by illness (**conditioned taste aversion**) or to prefer tastes that improve their health (**conditioned taste preference**)
   - in the wild these forms of learning are robust and adaptive, however in modern industrialized societies people eat so many different tastes in a day that their bodies cannot learn the relations between taste and outcome; thus people who live in the midst of plenty often suffer from malnutrition because their bodies cannot learn the relation between various tastes and their health-promoting or health-disrupting effects
   - for example, when **thiamin** (Vitamin B_1) deficient rats were offered three different diets, one of which had thiamin, within a few days all preferred the thiamin diet; however, when they were offered 10 new diets, few learned to consume the one with thiamin
   - recent research by Weingarten and his colleagues suggests that nondeprived humans and animals learn to become hungry when they are used to eating, not when they have an energy deficit--nondeprived humans and animals do not normally have energy deficits when they begin meals
   - Weingarten fed deprived rats 6 small meals per day of a highly palatable liquid diet at irregular intervals for 11 days; a buzzer-and-light conditional stimulus came on before each meal and stayed on during it
   - next, Weingarten gave these same rats continuous access to the palatable liquid diet; despite the fact that they consumed large quantities of the liquid diet throughout the day, each time the buzzer and light were presented the rats consumed a meal

6. **A Settling-Point Model of Body-Weight Regulation** *(use Digital Image Archive Figure CH10F14.BMP)*

   - the leaky-barrel model illustrates the ideas behind a **settling-point theory** of body weight regulation; in this model, the stability of body weight is the result of the stability of the various factors that influence energy intake and output; it accounts for the homeostasis of body weight without having to postulate a fixed set point, and it can also account for instances in which there are long-term changes in body weight, which a strict set-point model cannot
   - in this model, a permanent change in factors that influence energy intake or output produces a change in the settling point that is partially offset by negative feedback from other factors
   - How does the settling point model account for the following common weight-change scenarios? (1) A dieter loses 20 pounds, stops dieting, and regains the weight. (2) A dieter consumes exactly 1,000 calories per day; at first weight is lost at a rapid rate, but after a few months no more weight is lost. (3) A woman marries a professional cook; at first, she gains weight rapidly but eventually her weight stabilizes, and she can't seem to lose it.

Suggested Websites for Lecture 10a:

The Hypothalamus: *http://thalamus.wustl.edu/course/hypoANS.html*

From the Neuroscience Tutorial at Washington University's School of Medicine, a text-and-figure review of the anatomy, physiology, and function of the hypothalamus.

The Dynamics of Digestion: *http://www.sartek.com/HLWC/DOD.html*

From Luise Strehlow and the High Level Wellness page, an overview of ingestive behavior. Nice links to figures that complement the text; easy reading.

Recognizing and Treating Eating Disorders: *http://www.aabainc.org/home.html*

The home page for the American Anorexia and Bulimia Association. See also:

http://www.sciam.com/explorations/1998/030298eating/index.html
and
http://www.sciam.com/0896issue/0896gibbs.html

From Scientific American, two articles examining the neural bases of feeding, satiety, and eating disorders.

Lecture 10b

THE BIOPSYCHOLOGY OF DRINKING

Outline

1. Traditional View

2. Distribution of Fluid in the Body

3. Deprivation-Induced Drinking
    a. Cellular Dehydration
    b. Hypovolemia

4. Spontaneous Drinking
    a. Flavor
    b. Variety
    c. Learning

5. Satiety

Lecture Notes

1. **The Traditional View**

    -   traditionally, people have thought that drinking is motivated by a deficit in the body's water resources. Like eating, this idea of **deficit-induced** intake is sometimes true, but usually not. Before examining the factors that control drinking, we will examine the body's distribution of fluids

2. **Distribution of Fluid in the Body**
    -   to understand the regulation of fluids in the body, it is useful to think of the body as two fluid-filled compartments: an **intracellular compartment** and an **extracellular compartment**
    -   two-thirds of the body's water is inside cells; the one-third that is outside cells is distributed among interstitial fluid, blood, and cerebrospinal fluid
    -   normally the concentration of solutes in the fluids of the intracellular and extracellular compartments is the same (i.e., they are **isotonic**); when there is a concentration difference, water is drawn through cell membranes into the more concentrated solution until the difference disappears; the pressure that draws water from less concentrated (**hypotonic**) to more concentrated (**hypertonic**) solutions is called **osmotic pressure** (*use Digital Image Archive Figure CH10F16.BMP*)

3. **Deprivation-Induced Drinking** (*use Digital Image Archive Figure CH10F22.BMP*)

    -   when animals are deprived of water, two bodily fluid deficits are produced: **cellular dehydration** (reduction of water in cells) and **hypovolemia** (reduction of water in the blood); both deficits are factors in deprivation-induced drinking

    a. **Cellular Dehydration**
        -   cellular dehydration occurs when we are water deprived or when we eat a solute (e.g., sodium chloride) that does not pass into cells and thus draws water out of them; either treatment makes us thirsty; Where are the receptors that detect cellular dehydration and mediate thirst?
        -   injections of hypertonic saline into the carotid arteries in quantities that are too small to significantly influence the concentration of intracellular fluids outside the brain can induce drinking; this suggests that there are **osmoreceptors** in the brain
        -   the evidence suggest that cerebral osmoreceptors are located in the **lamina terminalis** and the **supraoptic area** of the diencephalon

b. **Hypovolemia**
   - hypovolemia is commonly induced in experiments by injecting **colloids** into the peritoneal cavity; colloids draw blood plasma into the peritoneal cavity, but they have little effect on the amount of water in cells
   - hypovolemia is detected by **baroreceptors** (blood pressure receptors) in the wall of the heart and **blood-flow receptors** in the kidneys
   - the activation of both the baroreceptors and the blood-flow receptors leads to the synthesis of the peptide hormone **angiotensin II**; angiotensin II is a **dipsogen**, a substance that induces drinking; Where in the brain does angiotensin II act to mediate hypovolemic drinking?
   - two general clues pointed to the **subfornical organ** (SFO), a midline structure just beneath the fornix on the roof of the third ventricle between the openings to the two lateral ventricles, as the sight of angiotensin action *(use Digital Image Archive Figure CH10F23.BMP)*
   - these two general clues were: (1) the SFO is one of only a small number of sites in the brain at which the blood-brain barrier does not greatly impede the entrance of angiotensin II; (2) injections of angiotensin II into the ventricles were extremely effective in eliciting drinking
   - four observations confirmed that angiotensin II receptors in the SFO mediate the dipsogenic effect of angiotensin II:

     (1) microinjection of angiotensin II into the SFO induced drinking;
     (2) **saralasin**, a blocker of angiotensin II receptors, blocked the dipsogenic effects of intraventricular angiotensin II injections;
     (3) SFO lesions blocked the dipsogenic effects of large IV angiotensin II injections; and
     (4) SFO neurons displayed dose-dependent increases in firing in response to injections of angiotensin II

4. **Spontaneous Drinking**

   - although research on the physiological mechanisms of drinking has focused almost exclusively on deprivation-induced drinking, in real-life situations we, and other animals living with ready access to water, rarely experience fluid deficits; almost all of our drinking occurs in the absence of fluid deficits
   - drinking in the absence of fluid deficits is called **spontaneous drinking**; it is influenced by a variety of factors; for example, by flavor, by variety, and by learning

a. **Flavor**
   - the fluid intake of rats skyrockets after a bit of **saccharin** is added to their water (note: Americans consume more soft drinks than water)
   - conversely, in one experiment a small amount of **quinine** was added to the water of rats for 60 days; there was a substantial decline of drinking but no signs of ill health
   - thus, rats with easy access to water appear to drink much more than they need, and they excrete the excess

b. **Variety**
   - drinking a particular beverage temporarily decreases its **incentive value**; thus, there is an increased preference for any continuously available fluid after it has been unavailable for a period of time; an example is the **saccharin elation effect** *(use Digital Image Archive Figure CH10F24.BMP);* if the saccharin solution is withdrawn for several days from the cages of rats who have had continuous access to both water and to the saccharin solution, there is an increase in the preference for the saccharin solution for 2 or 3 days following its return; similar elation effects have been demonstrated for other beverages (e.g., weak quinine solutions and alcohol solutions)
   - grossly excessive drinking (**polydipsia**) has been induced in rats by presenting them with a different flavored solution every 15 minutes
   - a small pellet of food every few minutes also induces massive amounts of drinking in rats; this is called **schedule-induced polydipsia**

    c.   **Learning**
- humans and animals learn to drink in **anticipation of deficits** (e.g., marathon runners); in one study, on each trial the odor of menthol was presented to rats just prior to a subcutaneous **formalin** injection, which induces temporary hypovolemia; after a few trials, the rats started drinking as soon as the menthol was presented

5. Satiety

- early researchers were strongly influenced by the idea that drinking is motivated by deviations from internal set points; thus they assumed that the factor responsible for terminating drinking was a return to an internal set point
- this theory meets with three problems: (1) most drinking begins in the absence of deficits; (2) most drinking stops long before substantial amounts of the fluid have been absorbed from the gut; and (3) when a fluid is very palatable people and animals drink far in excess of what they need to meet any fluid deficits they might have (e.g., the **saccharin elation effect).**
- the system seems to be designed to prevent water deficits, not just to respond to them; drinking is stimulated whenever palatable fluids are available, and excess fluids are simply excreted as dilute urine; fluid deficits do make us thirsty, but such deficits rarely occur in the everyday lives of most people

Suggested Websites for Lecture 10b:

    Polydipsia: *http://www.ndif.org/Abstract/jab-165.html*

        From the Nephrogenic Diabetes Insipidus Foundation, an information-loaded summary of polydipsia and NDI.

    Circumventricular Organs: *http://ecco.bsee.swin.edu.au/neuro/lumen/Circumventricular.html*

        From John McNulty's site at the Swinburne University of Technology, a text-and-figures page on the CVO and its role in drinking homeostasis.

    Water and Electrolyte Regulation: *http://www.usyd.edu.au/su/anaes/VAT/VATacid-base.html*

        From Ken Pauker at the University of Sydney, a comprehensive review of the structure and function of the kidney. For advanced students and instructors

Lecture 11a

THE NEUROENDOCRINE SYSTEM AND THE EFFECTS OF GONADAL HORMONES ON EARLY SEXUAL DIFFERENTIATION

Outline

1. The Neuroendocrine System
    a. Pituitary Gland
    b. Gonadal Hormones
    c. Control of the Pituitary by the Hypothalamus

2. Early Sexual Differentiation
    a. The "Mamawawa"
    b. Gonads
    c. Internal Reproductive Ducts
    d. External Reproductive Organs
    e. Brain Development
    f. Conclusion

Lecture Notes

1. The Neuroendocrine System

-   before I describe how hormones influence sexual development, I am going to introduce the fundamentals of neuroendocrine function, with an emphasis on the gonadal hormones

a. **Pituitary Gland** *(use Digital Image Archive Figure CH11F02.BMP)*
    -   the pituitary gland is often referred to as the "master gland" because it releases a variety of hormones, called **tropic hormones,** which travel through the blood to other glands and stimulate them to release hormones which have diverse, long-lasting effects
    -   the pituitary is in fact two glands: the **anterior pituitary** and the **posterior pituitary,** which dangle together from the pituitary stalk, which is attached to the **hypothalamus**
    -   strictly speaking, it is the anterior pituitary that is the master gland; only it releases tropic hormones

b. **Gonadal Hormones**
    -   within the context of sexual behavior, the **gonads** (the **testes** and the **ovaries**) are the most relevant targets of the anterior pituitary, and **gonadotropic hormones** are its most relevant hormones
    -   it is important to realize that both the ovaries and testes release exactly the same hormones, although they release them in different amounts during various stages of development
    -   the three major categories of gonadal hormones are: **estrogens** (e.g., estradiol), **androgens** (e.g., testosterone), and progestins (e.g., progesterone); the **adrenal cortex** releases the same hormones but in smaller amounts

c. **Control of the Pituitary by the Hypothalamus**
    -   a major difference between men and women is that gonadotropin release from the anterior pituitary cycles approximately every 28 days in women, but its release varies little from day to day in men; the release pattern for both sexes is **pulsatile**; attempts to understand this male-female difference led to an important discovery
    -   first, it was assumed that male and female pituitaries are fundamentally different (**steady vs. cyclic**), but female pituitaries implanted in males became "steady pituitaries", and male pituitaries implanted in females became "cyclic pituitaries"; this suggested that the pattern of anterior pituitary release was being controlled by another organ; it suggested that **"the master gland had its own master"**

- attention naturally turned to the hypothalamus, the neural structure to which the pituitary is connected; it was soon discovered that the hypothalamus controls the pituitary in two different ways: one way for the posterior pituitary and one for the anterior pituitary *(use Digital Image Archive Figure CH11F04.BMP)*

- axons of neurons in the **paraventricular** and **supraoptic** nuclei of the hypothalamus terminate in the posterior pituitary *(use Digital Image Archive Figure CH11F03.BMP)*
- **vasopressin** and **oxytocin** are synthesized in the cell bodies of these neurons, they are transported down their axons, and they are released from the posterior pituitary into general circulation; vasopressin facilitates reabsorption of water by the kidneys; oxytocin stimulates contractions of the uterus and ejection of milk in women (its function in males is unknown)

- the release of tropic hormones from the anterior pituitary is controlled by other hormones called **releasing hormones**; releasing hormones are released by the hypothalamus into the **hypothalamopituitary portal system**, which carries them to the anterior pituitary; gonadotropin-releasing hormone stimulates the release of the anterior pituitary's two **gonadotropins**: **follicle stimulating hormone** and **luteinizing hormone**

- in general, release of gonadal hormones is influenced by feedback; the feedback is usually negative, which maintains steady hormone levels; the hormone surges observed during **puberty** and in females just prior to **ovulation** seem to be associated with switches from a negative feedback mode to a positive feedback mode *(use Digital Image Archive Figure CH11F05.BMP)*

2. **Early Sexual Differentiation**

   a. **The "Mamawawa"**
      - the men-are-men-and-women-are-women assumption; there is a tendency to assume that men and women are distinct opposites; with respect to hormones, that men have male hormones that give them male bodies and brains and make them do male things, and that women have female hormones that give them female bodies and brains and make them do the opposite, i.e., female things
      - you will learn that virtually nothing about this fabled assumption is correct

   b. **Gonads**
      - the differentiation of male and female gonads occurs about 6 weeks after fertilization, at this time males and females have identical **primordial gonads**, each with two parts: a **medulla** and a **cortex**
      - in males (XY), the Y sex chromosome triggers the manufacture of a protein called **H-Y antigen**, which causes the medulla (core) of the primordial gonads to develop into testes
      - if no H-Y antigen is present (as in normal genetic females), the cortex of the primordial gonads naturally develops into ovaries
      - accordingly, genetic female fetuses injected with H-Y antigen develop testes, and genetic male fetuses injected with a drug that blocks H-Y antigen develop ovaries

   c. **Internal Reproductive Ducts**
      - 6 weeks after fertilization each fetus has two sets of undeveloped internal reproductive ducts, one male and one female; the undeveloped male system is called the **Wolffian system**; the undeveloped female system is called the **Müllerian System**
      - in normal genetic males, the testes release androgens in the third month and this causes the Wolffian system to develop; the testes also release **Müllerian-inhibiting substance**, which causes the Müllerian system to degenerate and the testes to descend into the scrotum; all fetuses exposed to androgen in the third month, whether genetic male or female, develop male ducts
      - any fetus, not exposed to androgens in the third month after conception (e.g., a normal genetic female, an ovariectomized genetic female, or an orchidectomized genetic male) will develop female reproductive ducts
      - **ovariectomy** refers specifically to removal of the ovaries; **orchidectomy** refers specifically to removal of the testes; **castration** and **gonadectomy** refer generally to removal of gonads

d. **External Reproductive Organs**
   - every normal human fetus begins with the precursors of both testes and ovaries and the precursors of both male and female internal reproductive ducts, but female and male fetuses have the same **bipotential precursor** of external reproductive organs
   - the surge of androgen release in the third month of fetal development causes this bipotential precursor to develop into male external genitals; in the absence of androgen it develops into female external genitals

e. **Brain Development**
   - there is growing evidence of differences between men and women in terms of **overall brain size**, the size of **specific structures** in the brain, and in **patterns of brain activity**
   - similar to the differentiation of other body organs, sexual differences in the brain appear to depend on exposure to high levels of androgens at **developmentally crucial times**
   - rats are a convenient species for the study of the sexual differentiation of the brain because when they are born, the period during which the development of their reproductive organs can be influenced by hormones has passed but the period during which the development of the brain is maximally influenced by hormones is just beginning
   - most research on brain differentiation has focused on the differentiation of the hypothalamus-controlled pattern of gonadotropin release into the steady male pattern or the female cyclic pattern
   - consistent with what you have already learned about reproductive-system development, rats exposed to androgens in the perinatal period (e.g., intact genetic male rats, intact genetic female rats injected with androgen, ovariectomized female rats injected with androgen) develop the steady, male pattern of gonadotropin release
   - in contrast, rats not exposed to androgen in the perinatal period (e.g., intact genetic female rats, ovariectomized genetic female rats, orchidectomized genetic male rats) develop the cyclic, female pattern of gonadotropin release
   - there is evidence to support the idea that in order to masculinize the rat brain testosterone must be converted to **estradiol**--a process called **aromatization**
   - the **aromatization hypothesis** is that testosterone released during the perinatal period enters the brain and is aromatized to estradiol and that it is actually estradiol that masculinizes the brain
   - four lines of evidence support this theory: (1) the **enzyme** necessary for aromatization is present in the neonatal rat, (2) **neonatal injections** of estradiol masculinize the rat brain, (3) **dihydrotestosterone**, a nonaromatizable androgen, does not masculinize the rat brain, and (4) agents that **block aromatization** block the masculinizing effects of neonatal testosterone injections
   - several documented differences between men and women have been seen in the brains of humans; men's brains are about **15% larger**, have a higher metabolic rate in the **temporal lobe** and **limbic system**; women have a more extensive **corpus callosum** and have higher metabolic activity in the **cingulate gyrus**; other differences are found in the anatomy of the hypothalamus, thalamus and anterior commisure
   - research is currently focusing on the functional significance of these differences

f. **Conclusion**

   - with respect to early development the "mamawawa" hypothesis is clearly incorrect; everybody is born with a female program of development; in normal males, the development of ovaries is overridden by H-Y antigen, and testes develop; then the androgens released by the testes override the program for the development of female reproductive organs and brains, and the male equivalents develop
   - hormone injections or gonadectomy at the appropriate stage of development can produce individuals whose bodily sex is different from their genetic sex; maleness and femaleness are but slight variations of the same, fundamentally female program of development

Suggested Websites for Lecture 11a:

Gender and Brain: *http://www.science.ca/scientists/Kimura/kimura.html*

A biography of sorts of Doreen Kimura, highlighting her work on sex differences in brain function.

Sexual Disorders Related to Pituitary Dysfunction: *http://medstat.med.utah.edu/kw/human_reprod/*

The homepage of the Pituitary Tumors Network Association; see their links to hormonal imbalances and to sexual and reproductive dysfunction.

Behavioral Neuroendocrinology: *http://www.sbne.org/*

Homepage for the Behavioral Neuroendocrinology Society and its journal, Hormones and Behavior.

84

Lecture 11b

THE EFFECTS OF SEX HORMONES IN
PUBERTY AND ADULTHOOD

Outline

1. The Role of Hormones in Pubertal Development
    a. Males
    b. Females

2. Effects of Hormones in Adulthood
    a. Males
    b. Females
    c. Anabolic Steroids

3. Androgenic Insensitivity Syndrome

4. The Hypothalamus and Sexual Behavior

5. Sexual Preference

Lecture Notes

1. **The Role of Hormones in Pubertal Development**

    - at the beginning of puberty, there is a surge in the release of **growth hormone** and of both the **gonadotropic hormones** from the anterior pituitary

    a. Males
    - in males the surge in **gonadotropic hormones** increases the release of **androgens** from the testes
    - this masculinizes the body; there is muscle development, body hair and pubic hair growth, lowering of the voice, the development of fertility, growth of sex organs, etc.

    b. Females
    - in females the pubertal surge of gonadotropin release stimulates the release of estrogens from the ovaries
    - this partially feminizes the body; estrogens stimulate breast growth, hip growth, onset of the menstrual cycle, fertility, etc.
    - the growth of pubic hair and axillary hair (underarm hair) is stimulated by **androstenedione**, an androgen released by the **adrenal cortex**, thus the "mamawawa" stumbles again

2. **Effects of Hormones in Adulthood**

    - hormones not only influence the **development** of the body and brain along male or female lines, they play a role in **activating** the sexual behavior of men and women

    a. Males
    - the role of androgens in activating the sexual behavior of adult males is apparent following **orchidectomy**
    - in about half the cases, there is a complete loss of ability to achieve an erection and of sexual motivation within a week or two of the operation; however, in other cases, the decline is less complete and/or more gradual; the reason for this variability is not understood
    - castrated men also exhibit a variety of physical changes, e.g., reduction of body hair, deposition of fat on hips and chest, softening of the skin, a marked reduction of strength

- **testosterone replacement injections** restore sexual motivation, sexual potency, and remasculinize the bodies of orchidectomized males; but they remain **sterile**
- the fact that testosterone injections restore the sexuality of orchidectomized males has led to the view that the sexual motivation and performance of a male is determined by his level of testosterone, and thus that these can be increased in healthy intact males by testosterone injections
- this is **NOT** the case; in healthy intact males there is no correlation between testosterone levels and sexuality, and substantial increases (e.g., by injection) or decreases (e.g., by **hemiorchidectomy**) in testosterone levels have no effect on sexual motivation or performance

    b. **Females**
- in female rodents, the 4 or 5 day menstrual cycle is correlated with a cycle of sexual receptivity (i.e., with an **estrous cycle**)
- in the day or two prior to ovulation, there is a gradual increase in estrogens, and a sudden surge in progesterone just as the mature egg is being released from its follicle
- during the next 12 to 18 hours the female is said to be in **estrus**: she is (1) **fertile**, (2) **receptive**, (3) **proceptive**, and (4) **sexually attractive** to male rats
- ovariectomy abolishes the estrous cycle; but ovariectomized female rodents can be readily brought into estrus by an injection of estradiol followed a day and a half later by an injection of progesterone
- human females are different; there is no clear-cut cycle of sexual receptivity associated with the menstrual cycle; ovariectomy eliminates vaginal lubrication, the menstrual cycle, and fertility, but it has no effect on sexual motivation
- according to one theory, the sexual motivation of human females is maintained by androgens; sexual motivation is lost following ovariectomy plus **adrenalectomy**, but is reinstated by replacement androgen injections; yet another slap in the face of the "mamawawa"

    c. **Anabolic Steroids**
- testosterone has **anabolic** (growth promoting) effects, but it is not a particularly effective anabolic agent because it is quickly broken down in the body
- chemists have synthesized similar chemicals belonging to the same class (steroids) that are not broken down so quickly; these are the so-called **anabolic steroids**; there is currently an epidemic of anabolic steroid abuse among athletes
- although the early experimental evidence was ambiguous, there is clear evidence that anabolic steroids can increase the muscularity, strength, and performance of both male and female athletes
- however, there are a number of devastating side-effects: **testicular atrophy** and **gynecomastia** (breast growth) have been reported in men; **amenorrhea**, sterility, **hirsutism** (excessive growth of body hair), growth of the clitoris, masculine body shape, baldness, and deepening of the voice have been reported in women; in both men and women, there have been reports of muscle pain, muscle spasms, excessive water retention, blood in the urine, acne, nausea, vomiting, bleeding of the tongue, fits of anger, fits of depression, and cancerous liver tumors

3. **Androgen Insensitivity Syndrome**

- in order to understand the important role of androgens in male development, it is informative to understand what happens to males in the absence of their effects; for example, there are otherwise normal genetic males who suffer from the **androgen insensitivity syndrome**; they have normal levels of androgen but their bodies do not respond to it
- genetic males with androgen insensitivity frequently come to the attention of a physician when they become concerned about their inability to get pregnant; they are ostensibly happily married women
- a physical examination reveals: (1) sparse pubic and axillary hair, (2) they do not menstruate, (3) they have shallow vaginas, (4) they have internal testes and undeveloped male internal reproductive ducts, and (5) their body cells are all of the normal male XY type

- How does this happen? Four steps appear to be involved:

    (1) At 6 weeks, **normal testes** develop under the control of the **Y chromosome.**
    (2) In the third month, testes release androgens, but normal female external reproductive organs (and presumably a female brain) develop because of the **androgen insensitivity**.
    (3) Also in the third month, their female internal reproductive ducts **degenerate** (e.g., the inner one-third of the vagina) under the influence of Müllerian-inhibiting substance, and their male internal reproductive ducts **do not develop** because of their androgen insensitivity.
    (4) At puberty, the low levels of estrogens released by the testes feminize the body because there are no offsetting androgen effects, but androstenedione cannot stimulate the female pattern of pubic and axillary hair growth.

- What treatment would you recommend? Typically, neither the patient nor the husband is informed of the nature of the problem; they are counseled to adopt; the vagina may be surgically enlarged to eliminate pain associated with intercourse

4. The Hypothalamus and Sexual Behavior *(use Digital Image Archive Figure CH11F02.BMP)*

- the role of the hypothalamus in the control of the pituitary gland led to an examination of sex differences in the hypothalamus
- notably, the **medial preoptic area** in rats was found to be several times larger in males than in females
- at birth, the medial preoptic area is the same size in both sexes; however, within the first few days postnatal this area grows rapidly in males but not females. This growth is stimulated by estradiol, aromatized from testosterone; castration a day-1 postnatal reduces the size of the medial preoptic in adult rats.
- the size of the medial preoptic area has been correlated with testosterone levels and some aspects of sexual behavior; furthermore, stimulation elicits male rat sexual behavior. However, bilateral lesions of the area have only slight effects on male rat sexual behavior.
- in female rats, the **ventromedial nucleus** of the thalamus contains circuits critical to sexual behavior; stimulation elicits these behaviors, and lesions there reduce it. The VMN is critical to the onset of estrus in female rats, as microinjections of estrogen and progesterone there will bring on estrus. The VMN appears to act via a projection to the **periaqueductal gray**.

5. Sexual Preference

- many humans are not **heterosexual**; they are sexually attracted to members of the same bodily sex (**homosexual**), or to members of both bodily sexes (**bisexual**)
- many people believe that sexual preference can be changed by castration or hormone injections
- however, in females neither castration nor hormone injections influence the direction or intensity of sexual motivation
- in males castration greatly reduces sexual motivation, but replacement injections simply reinstates the original intensity and direction of sexual preferences
- it is believed that the neural circuits underlying sexual preference are permanently established early in life as the result of the interaction between hormones and experience; for example, perinatal castration of males or testosterone treatment of females induces same-sex preferences in a variety of species
- this is difficult to prove, however; the experiments necessary to test this hypothesis cannot be ethically performed on humans, and homosexuality and bisexuality are difficult to model in nonhumans
- LeVay (1991) found that the **third interstitial nucleus of the hypothalamus** is more than twice as large in heterosexual males than it is in heterosexual females and homosexual males; however, it is not clear whether this difference was a cause or a product of the homosexual preferences of his subjects
- more recently, Hamer et al., (1993) found that the concordance rate for homosexuality was 52% in monozygotic twins and 22% in dizygotic twins, suggesting that there may be a genetic basis for homosexuality. A gene implicated in male sexual preference has been located on the X-chromosome.

Suggested Websites for Lecture 11b:

Androgen Insensitivity: *http://www.medhelp.org/www/ais/*

A page devoted to androgen insensitivity syndrome.

Is Homosexuality Genetic? An Interview with Simon LeVay:

http://bewell.com/healthy/sexuality/1998/ga/index.shtml

From the *Be Well* site, an interview with Dr. Simon LeVay about his research into neuroanatomical correlates of homosexuality.

Sex, Flies, and Genes: *http://www.sciam.com/0697issue/0697scicit4.html*

Evidence that sexual behavior is under a certain degree of genetic control...at least in fruit flies! From the Scientific American's *Science and the Citizen* page.

How the Brain Organizes Sexual Behavior: *http://www.epub.org.br/cm/n03/mente/sexo_i.htm*

Another good link to the Brain and Mind e-magazine from the State University of Campinas, Brazil; a review of the physiology of coitus and the influence that the brain has on sexual preference and its control of sexual behavior.

Lecture 12a

THE PHYSIOLOGICAL AND BEHAVIORAL CORRELATES
OF SLEEP AND DREAMING

Outline

1. Three Psychophysiological Measures of Sleep

2. The Five Stages of Sleep EEG

3. REM Sleep and Dreaming

4. Sleep Disorders
    a. Insomnia
    b. Hypersomnia
    c. REM-Sleep-Related Disorders

Lecture Notes

1. **Three Psychophysiological Measures of Sleep**

    -   in the 1930s, it was discovered that although **EEG** waves are generally high-voltage and slow during sleep, there are periods during sleep when they are similar to the low-voltage fast waves of wakefulness
    -   in 1953, Aserinsky and Kleitman discovered that **rapid eye movements** (REMs) occurred under the eyelids of sleeping subjects during the periods of low-voltage fast EEG activity
    -   in 1962, Berger and Oswald found that there was a dramatic decline of **EMG** activity in the muscles of the body core during these same sleep periods
    -   since these three discoveries, EEG, EOG (electrooculogram), and EMG have been monitored in most sleep experiments

2. **The Four Stages of Sleep EEG** *(use Digital Image Archive Figure CH12F02.BMP)*

    -   just before a subject falls asleep, the EEG is typically punctuated by bursts of alpha waves (large-amplitude, regular, 8-to-12-Hz waves indicative of relaxed wakefulness)
    -   when the subject falls asleep, the EEG progresses in sequence through initial stage 1, stage 2, stage 3, and stage 4

        -   **initial stage 1 sleep EEG** is low-voltage, fast activity similar to, but slightly slower than, that of wakefulness
        -   **stage 2 sleep EEG** is of higher voltage and slower than stage 1; its most obvious characteristics are **K complexes** (a single large negative wave followed by a single large positive wave) and **sleep spindles** (1-to-2-second waxing-and-waning bursts of 12-to-15-Hz waves)
        -   **stage 3 sleep EEG** is defined by the occasional presence of **delta waves**, the largest and slowest EEG waves (1 to 2 per second)
        -   **stage 4 sleep EEG** is defined by a predominance of delta waves

    -   once the sleeping subject has gone through initial stage 1 to stage 4, he or she goes back through the stages to stage 1 EEG
    -   but when the subject returns to stage 1 EEG, it is referred to as **emergent stage 1 EEG**, as it is every other time that the subject enters stage 1 during that night's sleep; it is called "emergent" stage 1 because it emerges from the other stages

- it is important to distinguish between initial stage 1 EEG and emergent stage 1 EEG because only emergent stage 1 EEG is associated with REMs and low levels of muscle tonus in core muscles
- the stage during which emergent stage 1 occurs is often called **REM sleep** or **paradoxical sleep**(it was initially considered a paradox that subjects slept while their EEGs suggested that they were awake); stages 2, 3, and 4 together are often referred to as **slow-wave sleep**; stages 3 and 4 together are often referred to as **delta sleep**
- the progression of EEG stages changes during a typical night's sleep; notice: (1) that each cycle is about 90 minutes long, (2) that as the night progresses less time is spent in stages 3 and 4 and more is spent in REM sleep, and (3) that there are brief periods of wakefulness, which are normally forgotten in the morning *(use Digital Image Archive Figure CH12F03.BMP)*

3. **REM Sleep and Dreaming**

- the discovery of REMs in 1953 by Kleitman and his colleagues led to the obvious hypothesis that REM-sleep periods were periods of dreaming; this hypothesis was confirmed by waking subjects up during various stages of sleep and asking them if they had been dreaming; about 80% of awakenings from REM sleep led to dream reports, and only 7% of awakenings from nonREM-sleep stages led to dream reports
- in the years since this discovery, a number of common beliefs about dreaming have been objectively tested by using EEG, EMG, and EOG indices of dreaming:

    (1) Are **external stimuli** incorporated into dream sequences? (yes, dripping water was in 14 out of 33 cases);
    (2) Do dreams run on **"real time"**? (yes, subjects awakened 5 or 15 minutes after the beginning of a dream could guess the correct interval on the basis of the contents of their dreams);
    (3) Does everybody dream? (yes, even people who claimed that they did not dream had normal amounts of REM, and they reported dreams if they were awakened during REM--although less frequently);
    (4) Are **penile erections** indicative of dreams with sexual content? (no, penile and clitoral tumescence occurs during all dreams, regardless of sexual content);
    (5) Are **somnambulism** and **sleep talking** the acting out of dreams? (no, they usually occur during stage 4);
    (6) Are dreams the **reliving** of stressful or sexual events of the previous day? (there is no good evidence for this)

- The Freudian theory of dreams, that dreams represent unacceptable wishes, was based on science and beliefs of the 1890's and has no support from today's science base
- Hobson's has proposed an **activation-synthesis theory** of dreaming, based upon the idea that the information passed on to the cortex during REM is random, and dreams are the cortex's effort to make sense of these random signals
- A few people have **lucid dreams** in which the dreamer knows that they are dreaming and can change the course of their dreams; lucid dreams are usually positive experiences

4. **Sleep Disorders**

- sleep disorders are of two major kinds: **insomnia** (complaints of too little sleep) and **hypersomnia** (complaints of too much sleep and tiredness)

a. **Insomnia**
- insomnia is often **iatrogenic** (physician induced); a person with minor difficulties in sleeping is often given sleeping pills (usually **benzodiazepines** such as Valium or Librium); **tolerance**develops to benzodiazepines so the patient starts to take larger and larger doses, and when they try to stop taking them, severe insomnia occurs as a withdrawal symptom; this causes them to return to their drug taking (see the case of Mr. B. in BIOPSYCHOLOGY); they become locked in a vicious circle
- another cause of insomnia is **sleep apnea**; in some patients, spasms of the throat muscles block air intake several times a night; if they do not recall their many awakenings, their excessive sleepiness the next day can lead to a diagnosis of hypersomnia

- **nocturnal myoclonus** is another cause of insomnia; subjects are briefly awakened each night by sudden twitches of the legs; it can lead to a diagnosis of hypersomnia if the patient does not recall the awakenings because he or she tends to be excessively sleepy during the day
- **restless legs** is a hard-to-describe tension in the legs that keeps people from falling asleep; this leads to a diagnosis of insomnia
- because benzodiazepines have muscle relaxant, anxiolytic, and anticonvulsive effects in addition to their hypnotic effects, they are often prescribed for nocturnal myoclonus and restless legs; unfortunately, they are rarely effective
- one large-scale study showed that people seeking help for insomnia claim that they sleep an average of 4.5 hours per night, but they actually sleep an average of 6.5 hours per night; it used to be the practice to assume that people who complained of insomnia but slept more than 6.5 hours per night were neurotic, and they were diagnosed as **pseudoinsomniacs**; this practice stopped when psychophysiological studies found that many of the people who had been diagnosed as neurotic were suffering from sleep-disturbing problems such as sleep apnea or nocturnal myoclonus; it seems that undisturbed sleep rather than sleep per se is what we need to feel rested the next day

b. **Hypersomnia**
- the most interesting disorder of hypersomnia is **narcolepsy**; narcoleptics tend to fall asleep in totally inappropriate situations (while having conversations, eating, or scuba diving), they usually sleep for 10 or 15 minutes and then awaken refreshed
- narcoleptics sleep only about one hour more per day than is average but often sleep at inappropriate times
- sleep promoting conditions are called **soporific**

c. **REM-Sleep-Related Disorders**
- narcoleptics go directly into REM sleep rather than going through other sleep stages, thus narcolepsy is often categorized with REM-sleep-related disorders
- **cataplexy** is commonly associated with narcolepsy; it is a sudden loss of muscle tone, sometimes triggered by an emotional event; in its extreme form, the sufferer drops as if shot and stays there for a minute or two while remaining conscious; the observation that narcoleptics, unlike normal people, go directly into REM sleep when they fall asleep has led to the view that a cataleptic attack is the muscle relaxation of REM sleep encroaching on wakefulness
- the **nucleus magnocellularis** of the caudal reticular formation normally becomes active during REM sleep to enforce muscle relaxation during dreaming; these cells become active during cataleptic attacks in dogs; presumably it is failure of the nucleus magnocellularis that causes the REM-sleep disorder in which people act out their dreams.
- hypersomnia is treated with **stimulants**; cataplexy is treated with **tricylic antidepressants** because they block REM sleep
- patients treated with tricyclic antidepressants and some individuals with brain damage do not experience REM sleep; there seem to be no adverse effects

Suggested Websites for Lecture 12a:

Sleep: *http://www.ninds.nih.gov/healinfo/DISORDER/SLEEP/brain-basics-sleep.HTM*

> for a comprehensive review of sleep, sleep stages, sleep pathology; complete with figures of EEG stages in sleep, neural structures involved in sleep, and dreaming and REM.

The Sleep Well: *http://www.stanford.edu/~dement/index.html*

> the site maintained by Dr. Daniel Dement, a pioneer in sleep research.

The Science of Sleep: *http://www.real.com/rafiles/npr/password/nf6m2201-5.ram*

> from National Public Radio, a RealTime audio interview with Dr. Clifford Saper, Dr. David White and Dr. Craig Heller on the Science of Sleep.

Lecture 12b

WHY DO WE SLEEP?

Outline

1. Why Do We Sleep?
   a. Recuperation Theory
   b. Circadian Theory

2. Circadian Sleep-Wake Cycles

3. The Effects of Sleep Reduction
   a. Total Sleep Deprivation
   b. REM-Sleep Deprivation
   c. Sleep Reduction

4. Recuperation and Circadian Models Combined

Lecture Notes

1. **Why Do We Sleep?**

   - all mammals and birds sleep; even fish, reptiles, amphibians, and insects go through periods of inactivity and unresponsiveness that are remarkably like mammalian sleep
   - this suggests that sleep fulfills some very important function, but what is it?

   a. Recuperation Theory
   - the essence of various **recuperation theories** of sleep is that being awake disrupts homeostasis in some way and that sleep is required to restore it
   - this is the way that most people think about sleep

   b. Circadian Theory
   - according to the **circadian theory** of sleep, sleep is not a response to an internal imbalance; sleep is an adaptive response that evolved to conserve energy and to protect organisms from mishap and predation; the urge to sleep evolved to be greatest during the night for animals who do not see well in dim illumination
   - the circadian theory of sleep considers sleep to be like sexual behavior; it is adaptive and there is a strong drive to engage in it, but its purpose is not to correct an inner deficiency

   - two lines of research have a direct bearing on whether sleep is fundamentally recuperative or circadian: (1) the study of circadian sleep cycles and (2) the study of the effects of sleep reduction

2. **Circadian Sleep-Wake Cycles**

   - almost every physiological function in surface-dwelling animals displays some kind of circadian rhythmicity; the sleep-wake cycle is the most obvious
   - the light-dark cycle is an important factor in the timing of most **circadian rhythms**; environmental cues (such as the light-dark cycle) that **entrain** circadian rhythms are called zeitgebers
   - however, sleep-wake cycles still cycle regularly in a constant environment; regular biological cycles in constant environments are called **free-running cycles**; the duration of a free-running cycle is its **free-running period**
   - *(use Digital Image Archive Figure CH12F03.BMP;* a free-running sleep-wake cycle of a man living in an unchanging environment; notice that the free-running period is 25.3 hours; free-running periods are usually greater than 24 hours)

- even animals raised from birth in unchanging laboratory environments display highly regular free-running cycles; circadian cycles thus do not appear to be learned
- the fact that such regularity is precisely maintained despite large day-to-day variations in physical and mental activity is strong support for the circadian theory of sleep; in fact, several studies have found a negative correlation between the length of a period of wakefulness and the length of the following period of sleep, even under free-running conditions *(use Digital Image Archive Figure CH12F06.BMP)*; this is the opposite of what the recuperation theory would predict; it seems that we are programmed to go to sleep every 24 hours or so and that if we stay awake longer than usual during a particular 24-hour cycle, there is less time left for sleep
- the **suprachiasmatic nuclei** (SCN) of the hypothalamus appear to contain the circadian timing mechanism; SCN lesions abolish most circadian cycles, and the neurons of the SCN display circadian patterns of activity
- light **zeitgebers** entrain circadian cycles via a path from the retina to the SCN, the **retinohypothalamic tract** *(use Digital Image Archive Figure CH12F16.BMP)*; lesions of the retinohypothalamic tract eliminate the ability of light to entrain circadian rhythms
- Alternating **shift work** and **jet lag** are situations where zeitgebers are phase advanced (moving to an earlier shift or flying east) or phase delayed (moving to a later shift or flying west); people must adjust their natural sleep-wake cycles or endure problems such as sleep disturbances, fatigue, and performance decrements; phase advances are more difficult adjustments than are phase delays

3. The Effects of Sleep Reduction

- the second line of research that has a direct bearing on the question of whether sleep is fundamentally circadian or recuperative is the research on sleep reduction
- the recuperation theory predicts: (1) that long periods of wakefulness will result in debilitating physiological deficits, (2) that these deficits will grow steadily worse as the sleep deprivation continues, and (3) that after the sleep deprivation has ended, much of the lost sleep will be regained

a. Total Deprivation

- the above predictions are seriously challenged by the documented cases of individuals such as Miss M., the elderly lady, who seemed to sleep only out of boredom--and then only about 1 hour per night
- there are also many studies in which subjects have been totally deprived of sleep for several days; these studies have not confirmed the predictions of the recuperation theory:

   (1) **no marked physiological disturbances** other than increased sleepiness have been discovered in sleep-deprived subjects although there have been many attempts to document them;
   (2) during sleep deprivation, subjects **do not become progressively more tired**; their sleepiness follows the usual circadian cycle, and there appears to be no increase in sleepiness after the third day;
   (3) after the termination of several days of total sleep deprivation, subjects sleep about 3 hours extra the first night and about an hour extra the next night, but then they return to their previous sleep schedule

- one might expect that sleep deprivation would produce severe performance deficits, particularly on complex tasks; study after study has shown this not to be the case; sleep-deprived subjects display some performance deficits but primarily on **boring, passive tasks**, requiring continuous attention; such deficits have been attributed to **microsleeps** (2-or-3-second periods during which subjects remain sitting or standing but their eyelids droop, they are unresponsive to external stimuli, and they have a sleep EEG)
- several experts who have reviewed the sleep-deprivation literature have reached the same general conclusion: "there is yet no evidence that sleep deprivation does anything to humans other than to increase their tendency to fall asleep"
- the recuperative theory also has difficulty explaining why some animals sleep so little (horses sleep 2 hours per day) while others sleep so much (cats sleep 14 hours per day and giant sloths sleep 20 hours per day)

b. **REM-Sleep Deprivation**

- because REM sleep is associated with dreaming, there has been much interest in the effects of the selective deprivation of REM sleep
- there are two major effects of REM sleep deprivation:

   (1) REM deprivation is enforced by waking subjects up each time that REMs begin to occur; as a period of REM deprivation progresses, subjects must be awakened more and more frequently to prevent them from having periods of REM sleep; and
   (2) after REM deprivation is curtailed, **REM rebound** is often seen; subjects get more than their normal amount of REM sleep for the next two or three nights

- one of the main challenges for anyone suggesting that REM sleep is critical to normal functioning must explain why **tricyclic antidepressants**, which block REM sleep at common therapeutic doses, produce but patients who have taken them regularly for years have experienced no adverse psychological side effects that can be attributed to REM deprivation

c. **Sleep Reduction**

- several studies have maintained subjects on programs of sleep-reduction
- a study by Friedman, Mullaney and their colleagues is the most thorough of such studies; 8 subjects were asked to reduce their sleep in 30-minute steps every few weeks until they felt that they did not want to reduce it further; then they slept at this shortest time for 1 month and at the shortest time plus 30 minutes for 2 months; finally, the subjects' natural sleep time was measured 1 year after they had returned to sleeping for as long as they pleased
- the results were: (1) the achieved minimum duration of nightly sleep was 5.5 hours for two subjects, 5.0 hours for four subjects and 4.5 hours for two subjects; (2) there was a major **increase in sleep efficiency** (less time to fall asleep, fewer awakenings, more stage 4 sleep); (3) there were **no deficits** on any of the numerous performance and psychological tests given throughout the experiment; (4) a year after the period of sleep restriction, all subjects were naturally sleeping between 7 and 18 hours less per week

4. **Recuperation and Circadian Models Combined** *(use Digital Image Archive Figure CH12F10.BMP)*

- experimental evidence seems to come down strongly in favor of the circadian theory but several recent findings support the theory that both circadian and recuperative factors are important; thus some of the sleep that we get may serve a recuperative function, and some simply serves to conserve energy and keep us safe
- support for this combination theory has taken a long time to accumulate because in most sleep-deprivation studies only the total duration of sleep has been recorded, rather than the duration of the various sleep stages
- the following lines of evidence suggest that slow-wave sleep serves a recuperative function but that stage 2 and REM sleep do not:

   (1) sleep-deprived subjects regain much of their lost stage 4 sleep after the period of deprivation;
   (2) subjects who reduce their sleep time do so by reducing their REM sleep and stage 2 sleep;
   (3) short sleepers typically get as much stage 3 and stage 4 sleep as long sleepers;
   (4) extra sleep obtained in the morning contains almost no stages 3 and 4, and it does not reduce the time spent sleeping the next night;
   (5) after sleep deprivation, the proportion of slow waves in the EEG is higher

- the evidence from sleep-reduction studies suggests that most individuals can adapt to sleep schedules of about 5½ hours per night
- What do you think of this conclusion? Do you think that it would be worth the effort of reducing your sleep time to create more waking hours for yourself? What kind of individuals would have the least difficulty reducing their sleep time?
- How might you rearrange your schedule during the day to make sleep reduction more feasible?

Suggested Websites for Lecture 12b:

Biological and Circadian Rhythms: *http://www.epub.org.br/cm/n04/mente/cloks_i.htm*

> From the Brain and Mind site, an overview of the neural structures involved in establishing circadian rhythms; good figures, and links to related sites. See also:

> *http://www.sfu.ca/~mcantle/rhythms.html*

> From Dr. Ralph Mistleberger at Simon Fraser University; see the overview of biological rhythms and his links to other "sites with rhythm". You might also look at:

> *http://www.srbr.org/*

> the site maintained by the Society for Research on Biological Rhythms.

Sleep Deprivation: *http://www.mhsource.com/edu/psytimes/p980301b.html*

> A provocative article by Dr. Stanley Cohen, highlighting the possible negative effects of long-term sleep deprivation.

Melatonin and Sleep: *http://www.sciam.com/explorations/040196explorations.html*

> From Scientific American, a critical look at the "drug of darkness", the neurohormone and putative sleep aid melatonin.

Lecture 13a

PRINCIPLES OF DRUG ACTION

Outline

1. The Drug Problem

2. Routes of Drug Administration

3. Mechanisms of Psychoactive Drug Action

4. Drug Tolerance
   a. Contingent Drug Tolerance
   b. Conditioned Drug Tolerance

5. Withdrawal Symptoms

6. Addiction, Physical Dependence, and Psychological Dependence

Lecture Notes

1. The Drug Problem

- 60 million people in the USA alone are addicted to alcohol, nicotine or both; 5.5 million are addicted to illegal drugs and millions to legal pharmaceuticals
- it is important to note at the outset that the legal status of a drug says nothing about its safety or the health risks associated with it…for the most part, a drug's legal status was determined before we knew much about the risks associated with it

2. Routes of Drug Administration

- drugs are consumed by people in the following ways:
- **ingestion;** swallowing drugs is convenient but a major drawback is that the timing and magnitude of the drug effects are greatly influenced by food in the stomach; some drugs are deactivated before they can be absorbed from the digestive tract and thus cannot be administered by this route; most drugs are absorbed from the **small intenstine,** but those with small molecules (e.g., alcohol) can be absorbed through the stomach wall, and thus they act more rapidly
- **inhalation;** many inhaled chemicals are absorbed directly into the bloodstream from the lungs (e.g., chemicals in tobacco and marijuana smoke); lung damage is a serious risk from the repeated inhalation of chemicals
- **mucous membranes;** some drugs (e.g., cocaine) are readily absorbed through the mucous membranes of the nose, mouth, or rectum; this method of administration is problematic as these membranes can be easily damaged
- **injection; SC, IM,** or **IV**; addicts typically favor the IV route, which is particularly dangerous; because it is fast and direct, there is a risk of death from overdose, impure drugs, or allergic reactions; there are only a few sites on the body appropriate for IV injection, thus addicts frequently develop infections and scar tissue at these sites

3. Mechanisms of Psychoactive Drug Action

- in order to produce psychoactive effects, drugs must enter the nervous system; fortunately, many drugs that are potentially dangerous neurotoxins do not readily penetrate the neurons of the CNS due to the **blood-brain barrier**; it is mediated by the particularly small pores in the walls of CNS blood vessels
- once a psychoactive drug has penetrated the CNS, it can influence neural activity in numerous ways; e.g., it can act diffusely on neural membranes or interact specifically with particular classes of neurotransmitters and receptors
- the effects of psychoactive drugs are terminated by their **metabolism,** i.e., by their conversion to nonactive **metabolites**; most drugs are metabolized by **liver enzymes**, only small amounts of unmetabolized active drugs are eliminated in sweat, breath, urine, etc.

4. Drug Tolerance *(use Digital Image Archive Figure CH13F02.BMP)*

- **drug tolerance** is any diminution of a drug's effect that results from prior exposure to the drug
- tolerance can be measured in two ways: (1) by measuring the decrease in the response elicited by the same dose of the drug, or (2) by measuring the increase in the amount of drug required to produce the same effect; in effect, drug tolerance is a shift in the **dose-response curve** to the right
- it is common to think of tolerance effects as being of two different types:
    - (1) **metabolic tolerance** (any tolerance effect that results from a decrease in the amount of the drug reaching the target cells) or
    - (2) **functional tolerance** (any tolerance that results from a decrease in the ability of the drug to influence the target cells)
- tolerance to most psychoactive drugs is primarily functional; an important thing to remember about functional tolerance is that it often develops for some effects of a drug but not others
- this specificity is difficult to explain in terms of the traditional idea that tolerance development is influenced entirely by drug-exposure-related variables such as the route, the dose, and the frequency of drug administration
- this **drug-exposure** view of tolerance has been seriously undermined by two different lines of psychopharmacological research: (1) **contingent tolerance** research has focused on the role of the subjects' behavior during drug exposure on the development of tolerance, and (2) **conditioned tolerance** research has focused on the role of the environment in which the drug is administered on the development of tolerance

a. Contingent Drug Tolerance

- contingent drug tolerance is any drug-tolerance effect that is contingent on the occurrence of a particular experience or behavior while the subject is under the influence of the drug; it is usually demonstrated by **before-and-after experiments**
- in before-and-after experiments, the subjects in one condition (the **drug-before-test condition**) are tested after each injection so that they repeatedly experience the effect of the drug on the test behavior; the subjects in the other condition (the **drug-after-test condition**) are tested before each injection so that they do not repeatedly experience the drug's effect on the test behavior
- the typical finding in such experiments is that tolerance is substantially greater in the drug-before-test condition than in the drug-after-test condition
- for example, Pinel et al. demonstrated contingent tolerance to the anticonvulsant effect of alcohol *(use Digital Image Archive Figure CH13F04.BMP).*
- During the tolerance-development phase of this experiment, the rats in one group received an alcohol injection once every 48 hours, 1 hour before a convulsive amygdala stimulation, thus they repeatedly experienced alcohol's anticonvulsant effect; the rats in the other group received alcohol injections on the same bi-daily schedule, but 1 hour after each convulsive stimulation, thus they never experienced alcohol's anticonvulsant effect; on the test day, only the rats in the **alcohol-before-stimulation group** were tolerant to alcohol's anticonvulsant effect
- the numerous reports of various contingent tolerance effects supports the idea that functional drug tolerance is an adaptation to the drug's effects on ongoing neural activity, rather than to the mere exposure of the nervous system to the drug; for example, it is the experience of alcohol's anticonvulsant effect that leads to the development of tolerance to it, not the mere exposure to alcohol

b. Conditioned Drug Tolerance

- **conditioned drug tolerance** refers to any tolerance effect that develops only in the presence of drug-predictive stimuli; the main support for the idea that drug tolerance can be conditioned comes from demonstrations of **situationally specific tolerance**
- for example; Crowell, Hinson, and Siegel (1981) demonstrated conditioned tolerance to the **hypothermic** effect of alcohol (*Digital Image Archive Figure CH13F05.BMP*). In this study, two groups of rats received 20 alcohol injections and 20 saline injections in alternating sequence, one every 48 hours; the only difference between the two groups was that the rats in one group always received their alcohol in a distinctive test room and their saline in their colony room, whereas the rats in the other group received their saline in the test room and their alcohol in the colony room; remarkably, tolerance to the hypothermic effect of alcohol was revealed only when the subjects were tested in the same environment in which they had previously received alcohol
- according to Siegel, Hinson, Krank, and McCully (1982), addicts develop tolerance to drug effects repeatedly experienced in the same environment and consequently start taking more of the drug, but when they take the elevated dose in a novel environment in which they are not tolerant, they run the risk of a **drug overdose**; in support of this hypothesis, Siegel et al. showed that rats were more susceptible to the lethal effects of a heroin overdose if they received the injection in an environment different from that in which they had experienced the effects of previous drug injections
- one theory of the situational specificity of tolerance is Siegel's **conditioned compensatory response theory**; Siegel proposed that each incidence of drug administration is like a Pavlovian conditioning trial; the drug effect is the UCS, which is preceded on each trial by the drug-environment CS; as the conditioning occurs, the drug-environment CS begins to elicit CRs that are opposite to the effects of the drug; these **conditioned compensatory responses**--as Siegel termed them--offset the effects of the drug, and tolerance is the consequence
- in support of this theory, several experiments have shown that drug tolerance can be **extinguished** by repeatedly presenting the drug-predictive environment, without the drug

5. Withdrawal Symptoms

- after large amounts of a drug have been in the body more or less continuously for a day or two, its sudden elimination can lead to **withdrawal symptoms**, which are typically opposite to the effects of the drug (e.g., anticonvulsant drugs such as alcohol and barbiturates typically induce epileptic withdrawal effects and sleeping pills typically induce insomnia if they are suddenly withdrawn)
- tolerance and withdrawal are thought to be different manifestations of the same underlying physiological change (*Digital Image Archive Figure CH13F03.BMP*); when the drug is removed, the drug-offsetting physiological changes that are the basis of tolerance, are no longer held in check by the drug, and withdrawal symptoms opposite to the original effects of the drug are the result

6. Addiction, Physical Dependence, and Psychological Dependence

- not all drug users are addicts; addicts are drug users who habitually use a drug despite their efforts to stop and despite its adverse effects on their health and social life
- individuals who display withdrawal symptoms if their drug are withheld are said to be **physically dependent**; most people think that only hard-core addicts are physically dependent, but if you have experienced a **hangover**, you have been physically dependent on alcohol; a hangover is a mild alcohol withdrawal syndrome
- early theories attributed drug addiction to physical dependence; the addict was seen as someone trapped by the need to keep taking the drug to prevent withdrawal symptoms; thus, early treatment programs were based on the idea that addicts could be cured by hospitalizing them until all of the drug was out of their system and all of their withdrawal effects had subsided
- however, this approach has proven to be almost totally ineffective; it is now clear that addicts are motivated to take their drug even after they have been **detoxified**; addiction in the absence of physical dependence is sometimes referred to as **psychological dependence**; by this definition, every addict displays substantial psychological dependence

- research is now focused on addicts who are motivated primarily by the anticipated pleasurable effects of their drugs; this view of addiction is called the **positive-incentive theory**. According to the positive-incentive theory of drug addiction (which is similar to the positive-incentive theory of feeding that you have already encountered), drugs may sometimes be taken to avoid withdrawal symptoms but it is much more often the case that they are ingested because the addict is seeking their pleasurable consequences. This idea will be explored more fully in the next lecture.

Suggested Websites for Lecture 13a

Neural Bases of Addiction:

http://www.med.harvard.edu/publications/On_The_Brain/Volume2/Special/SPAdd.html

An interview with Dr. Steven Hyman and Dr. Howard Shaffer on the neural bases of addiction; from Harvard University's Mahoney Neuroscience Institute. See also:

http://wings.buffalo.edu/aru/ARUbiological.htm

a site from the University of Buffalo's Addiction Research Unit; complete with animations and links to related pages.

Lecture 13b

DRUG ADDICTION, REWARDING BRAIN STIMULATION, AND THE
MESOTELENCEPHALIC DOPAMINE SYSTEM

Outline

1. Commonly Abused Drugs

2. Physical-Dependence Theories of Addiction

3. Positive-Incentive Theories of Addiction

4. Intracranial Self-Stimulation
    a. Fundamental Features
    b. Mesotelencephalic Dopamine System

5. The Mesotelencephalic Dopamine System and Drug Self-Administration

Lecture Notes

1. Commonly Abused Drugs

-   **Tobacco** is used more than any other drug except caffeine; usually inhaled or absorbed through oral mucosa; **nicotine** is the major psychoactive ingredient; 4,000 other known chemicals are in tobacco; tobacco is **highly addictive** (e.g., patients with **Buerger's disease** will still smoke, even after their limbs are amputated); effects ranging from nausea to relaxation; consequences of smoking range from coughing to failure of the cardiorespiratory system to cancer

-   **Alcohol** is consumed by 66% of the US population and 15 million are addicted; orally ingested; at most doses it is a **depressant** resulting in impaired function and is implicated in almost 50% of traffic fatalities; is believed to act primarily at the **GABA-A** receptor complex; alcohol is a small molecule and thus crosses the blood-brain barrier resulting in brain damage such as seen in **Korsakoff's** syndrome; alcohol also crosses the placenta and can result in birth defects such as **Fetal Alcohol Syndrome.** Very severe withdrawal effects; **delerium tremens** represent the 3rd stage of withdrawal, and may be lethal.

-   **Marijuana** elicits psychoactive responses largely due to **THC** may be inhaled or ingested orally (usually baked into an oil-rich substrate to aid absorption); act at THC receptors throughout the brain; effects range from craving sweets to very relaxed states to periods of impaired judgement and short-term memory impairment; a possible negative consequence is lung damage due to inhaling the drug; clinically, marijuana has been shown to block the nausea of cancer drugs, stimulate appetite, and decrease the severity of **glaucoma**

-   **Cocaine** and other stimulants have the same general effect, but differ greatly in their potency; may be inhaled, absorbed across mucosal membranes, or ingested orally; cocaine is very addictive; it acts by blocking catecholamine reuptake; it is a general stimulant, producing a feeling of energy, well-being, and self-confidence; extremely high doses can lead to **cocaine psychosis** characterized by sleeplessness, nausea, restlessness and psychotic behavior. Very high doses can produce stroke, seizures, and respiratory arrest; withdrawal symptoms are mild. Clinically, cocaine derivatives are effective as local anesthetics

- **Opiates** include morphine and heroin; these are unmatched as **analgesics** and are very addictive; act at receptors for **endogenous opiate neurotransmitters** that are located throughout the brain; elicits moderately severe withdrawal symptoms but these are not lethal; over 2 million Americans use heroin to experience a rush of pleasure and drowsy euphoria; tolerance leads to an ever greater use of the drug which has many crime implications; outside of IV transmitted diseases and problems, very **few health risks** are seen in users

2. Physical-Dependence Theories of Addiction

- addicts almost always return to drug taking after they have been released from hospital
- the failure of this treatment approach is not surprising in the light of two well-established facts about drug taking: (1) some highly addictive drugs produce little withdrawal distress (e.g., cocaine), (2) the pattern of drug taking in many addicts typically involves self-imposed cycles of **binges** and **detoxification**
- modern **physical-dependence theories** of addiction attempt to account for the inevitability of relapse after detoxification by postulating that withdrawal effects can be conditioned; there are two problems with this theory: (1) many of the conditioned effects elicited by drug-taking environments are similar to the effects of the drug, not to the drug's withdrawal effects; (2) addicts and experimental animals often find drug-related cues rewarding, even in the absence of the drug (e.g., **needle freaks** enjoy sticking empty hypodermic needles in their arms)

3. Positive-Incentive Theories of Addiction

- the failings of physical-dependence theories have lent support to **positive-incentive theories**; according to positive-incentive theories of addiction, most addicts take drugs to obtain their pleasurable effects rather than to escape their aversive aftereffects
- Robinson and Berridge (1993) have suggested that the expectation of the pleasurable effects of drugs may become **sensitized** in addicts; a key point of this **incentive-sensitization** theory is that addicts don't receive more pleasure from the drug, it is the **anticipated pleasure** that motivates their behavior.
- the positive-incentive theories of addiction led investigators interested in the physiological bases of addiction to consider what was known about the physiological systems in the brain that subserve the experience of pleasure and reward
- since the early 1950s, the physiological bases of pleasure have been investigated by studying the rewarding effects of electrical stimulation to various parts of the brain; these rewarding effects are measured by determining the degree to which rats will press a lever to deliver electrical stimulation to certain areas of their own brains (the **intracranial self-stimulation paradigm**)

4. Intracranial Self-Stimulation (ICSS)

- ICSS was discovered by accident in the early 1950s by Olds and Milner
- although animals self-stimulate a variety of brain structures, most studies in the 1950s and 1960s focused on the **septum** and **lateral hypothalamus** because the self-stimulation rates at these sites are impressively high

a. Fundamental Features of ICSS

- early studies suggested that lever pressing for brain stimulation was fundamentally different from lever pressing for food or water; ICSS was often characterized by (1) extremely **high response rates**, (2) **rapid extinction**, and (3) **priming**; these and other differences appeared to discredit Olds and Milner's original premise that animals self-stimulate sites that activate natural reward circuits (e.g., circuits that normally mediate the rewarding effects of food, water, sex, etc.)
- the pendulum of scientific opinion has swung as evidence has accumulated linking intracranial self-stimulation to natural reward mechanisms

- four lines of evidence have linked intracranial self-stimulation to natural reward mechanisms:

    (1) in the presence of the appropriate goal objects, stimulation at positive self-stimulation sites often elicits natural motivated behaviors such as eating, drinking, and copulation;
    (2) increasing levels of natural motivation (e.g., by food or water deprivation) often increases self-stimulation rates;
    (3) self-stimulation at sites other than the septum and lateral hypothalamus is frequently similar to lever pressing for natural reinforcers (e.g., slower response rates, slower extinction, no priming); and
    (4) subtle differences between the paradigm used to assess lever pressing for natural reinforcers and the paradigm used to assess lever pressing for brain stimulation contributed to the impression that the rewarding effects of brain stimulation and those of natural reinforcers were fundamentally different

- Panksepp and Trowill (1967) pointed out that in contrast to rats' lever pressing for food, self-stimulating rats are not deprived and they don't have to perform an additional **consummatory response** (e.g., eating) after each lever press to obtain the reinforcement; Panksepp and Trowill showed that nondeprived rats' lever pressing to inject small amounts of chocolate milk directly into their mouths through an implanted tube, performed remarkably like self-stimulating rats: (1) they learned very rapidly to lever press, (2) they extinguished almost immediately, and (3) some even had to be primed

b. Mesotelencephalic Dopamine System

- a variety of neural circuits can mediate self-stimulation but one neural system that appears to play a particularly important role is **the mesotelencephalic dopamine system** *(use Digital Image Archive Figure CH13F10.BMP)*
- the mesotelencephalic dopamine system ascends from two mesencephalic dopaminergic nuclei: the **substantia nigra** and the **ventral tegmental area**; at one time it was thought that all of the axons of substantia nigra neurons terminated in the striatum and they were commonly referred to as the **nigrostriatal pathway** (which we have discussed with respect to Parkinson's disease); similarly, it was thought that all of the axons of ventral tegmental area neurons projected to the limbic system and cortex (hence the name **mesocortical limbic pathway**). Recent findings indicate that there is considerably more intermingling between these two dopamine pathways than was once thought, and it has become common to refer to them together as the mesotelencephalic dopamine system
- four kinds of evidence support the notion that the mesotelencephalic dopamine system plays a particularly important role in self-stimulation:

    (1) **Mapping Studies:** areas that support ICSS are typically part of the mesotelencephalic dopamine system or else project there *(use Digital Image Archive Figure CH13F09.BMP)*;
    (2) *In vivo* **Cerebral Microdialysis Studies:** Phillips and his colleagues have demonstrated an increase in the release of dopamine from the mesotelencephalic dopamine system when an animal is engaged in ICSS *(use Digital Image Archive Figure CH13F11.BMP)*;
    (3) **Dopamine Agonist and Antagonist Studies:** it has been shown that dopamine agonists increase ICSS and dopamine antagonists decrease ICSS; and
    (4) **Lesion Studies:** lesions of the mesotelencephalic dopamine system disrupt ICSS.

5. The Mesotelencephalic Dopamine System and Drug Addiction

- the most **isomorphic** animal model of human addiction is the **drug self-administration paradigm** *(use Digital Image Archive Figure CH13F12.BMP)*; animals will self-administer many addictive drugs, often mimicking many of the drug-taking behaviors characteristic of human addicts
- the **conditioned place-preference paradigm** is also used to examine the rewarding effects of drugs;
- during the conditioning phase, rats repeatedly receive a drug in the **drug compartment** of a two-compartment box; during testing, drug-free rats are placed in the box and the proportion of time spent in the compartment where it used   to receive the drug is compared to time spent in the control compartment

102

- during drug-free testing rats spend more time in the drug compartment
- Using ICSS, self-administration and place-prefence conditioning paradigms, investigators have established five major lines of evidence support the view that the mesotelencephalic dopamine system, particularly its mesocortical-limbic division, mediates the rewarding effects of drugs:

(1) laboratory animals self-administer microinjections of addictive drugs into various structures of the mesotelencephalic dopamine system but usually not into other brain areas;
(2) microinjections of drugs into various structures of the mesotelencephalic dopamine system lead to the development of conditioned place-preferences;
(3) addictive drugs have been shown to increase the rewarding effects of electrical stimulation to the mesotelencephalic dopamine system, whereas nonaddictive drugs do not;
(4) destruction of mesotelencephalic function by lesions or dopamine antagonists has been shown to reduce the rewarding effects of addictive drugs; and
(5) systemic self-administration of most addictive drugs is associated with increased dopamine release from the nucleus accumbens, the striatum and other terminals of the mesotelencephalic system

Conclusion: current evidence suggests that the mesotelencephalic dopamine system can mediate the rewarding effects of some addictive drugs; thus, it may eventually prove possible to help those addicts who wish to give up their habit by the pharmacological manipulation of this system

Suggested Websites for Lecture 13b:

Ethanol: *http://www.dana.org/dabi/db_33.html*

From the Dana Foundation, an overview of the effects of ethanol on the nervous system; includes information about Korsakoff's syndrome.

Heroin: *http://www.nida.nih.gov/ResearchReports/Heroin/Heroin.html*

From NIDA, a monograph on heroin/opiate addiction.

Marijuana: *http://www.nida.nih.gov/Infofax/marijuana.html*

General information about the health consequences of marijuana; good recent statistics.

Nicotine: *http://www.nida.nih.gov/ResearchReports/Nicotine/Nicotine.html*

From NIDA, a monograph on nicotine; simply written, many up-to-date statistics.

Addiction Research Foundation: *http://www.arf.org/*

A good source of educational material about drugs and drug abuse.

Brookhaven National Laboratory's Images of Addiction: *http://www.pet.bnl.gov/images.html*

A collection of animations, PET images, and other images illustrating the effects of cocaine, nicotine, and other drugs of abuse on the brain. Highly recommended

Lecture 14a

THE NEUROPSYCHOLOGY OF MEDIAL-TEMPORAL-LOBE
AND MEDIAL-DIENCEPHALIC AMNESIA

Outline

1. The Case of H.M.
   a. The Surgery
   b. H.M.'s Memory Deficits
   c. Impact of H.M.'s Case

2. The Case of R.B.

3. Korsakoff's Amnesia

4. The Case of N.A.

5. Memory Deficits and Prefrontal Cortex Damage

6. Alzheimer's Disease

7. Posttraumatic Amnesia

Lecture Notes

- In general **memory** refers to brain activity that stores the effects of experience; we have learned much about the neural mechanisms of memory by studying amnesic patients

1. **The Case of H.M.**

   - H.M. suffered from severe, intractable epilepsy; he seemed to have **epileptic foci** in both **medial temporal lobes**

   a. **The Surgery**
      - because unilateral medial temporal lobectomy had proven successful in patients with one focus, a **bilateral medial temporal lobectomy** was prescribed for H.M.; this included the removal of the **hippocampus** and **amygdala** *(use Digital Image Archive Figure CH14F02.BMP)*
      - in some respects, the operation was a success: (1) his convulsions were reduced in severity and frequency, (2) his I.Q. increased from about 104 to about 118, (3) he remained an emotionally stable individual with generally superior psychological abilities
      - there is one exception to this otherwise rosy picture

   b. **H.M.'s memory deficits**
      - H.M. has minor **retrograde amnesia** (amnesia for events before his surgery) for events of the 2 years preceding the surgery; he has normal memory for remote events; he has normal **short-term memory** (his digit span is about 6); however, he cannot form long-term memories for events that occurred after his surgery (**anterograde amnesia**), for example he has no memory of his new home, his new job, or new friends (see chapter 14 in BIOPSYCHOLOGY)
      - at first, it was assumed that H.M. could not form long-term memories at all, but objective testing revealed that H.M. can demonstrate his retention of certain types of tasks by his improved performance on them, although he has **no conscious recollection** of previously practicing them

104

- the following was H.M.'s performance on six objective tests of memory:

  - **Digit Span +1 Test:** after 25 trials with the same series of digits, he could do only 7 digits, just one more than his normal memory span
  - **Block-Tapping Memory-Span Test:** his block-tapping memory-span was normal; but he could not extend it, even by one, when the same sequence was repeated for 12 trials
  - **Matching-to-Sample Tests:** he retained **rehearsable** (verbal) items for 40 seconds (the longest interval tested), but could not retain **nonrehearsable** items (various ellipses) for more than 5 seconds; control subjects retained all items perfectly *(use Digital Image Archive Figure CH14F03.BMP)*
  - **Mirror-Drawing Test:** he displayed substantial savings with no conscious recall of previous practice
  - **Rotary-Pursuit Test:** he displayed substantial savings with no conscious recall of previous practice
  - **Incomplete-Pictures Test:** after seeing 5 sets of 20 line drawings of varying completeness, he displayed substantial savings with no conscious recall of the drawings *(use Digital Image Archive Figure CH14F06.BMP)*
  - **Pavlovian Conditioning:** tones and a puff of air to the eye were presented to H.M.; he blinked in response; two years later he retained this conditioned pairing almost perfectly although he had no conscious awareness of his previous training

c. **Impact of H.M.'s Case**

- H.M.'s case had the following significant influences on the study of memory:

  (1) H.M.'s deficits were initially attributed to his hippocampal damage; it was the first case to implicate the hippocampus in memory; more significantly, H.M.s case refuted Lashley's **principle of equipotentiality** (all parts of the neocortex playing a role in memory);
  (2) H.M.'s case challenged the view that mnemonic functions are diffusely represented throughout the forebrain as well as challenging specific location concepts such as Lashley's engram (a specific brain change responsible for storing a memory);
  (3) H.M.'s case provided the first strong evidence that there is a different mode of storage for **short-term** and **long-term** memories;
  (4) H.M.'s case provided the first evidence that **implicit memory** could survive in the absence of **explicit memory;**
  (5) H.M.'s case suggested that the medial temporal lobes were involved in transferring information from short to long term memory, this is called **consolidation;**
  (6) H.M.'s 2-year gradient of retrograde amnesia suggested that consolidation is not mediated by **reverberatory neural activity** (neural reverberation could not possibly last for 2 years) but is mediated by the medial temporal lobes

2. **The Case of R.B.** *(use Digital Image Archive Figure CH14F07.BMP)*

- R.B. suffered **ischemia**-produced brain damage during heart surgery; subsequently, R.B. displayed a pattern of amnesic deficits similar to, although less severe than, that of H.M.
- shortly after testing, R.B. died and postmortem examination revealed damage to the **pyramidal cell layer** of the **CA1 hippocampal subfield,** but no other obvious damage
- this supported the original hypothesis that H.M.'s deficits were attributable to his hippocampal damage, rather than to damage to other medial-temporal-lobe structures
- however, it is impossible to rule out the possibility that there were subtle anatomical or functional disturbances in other parts of R.B.'s brain

3. **Korsakoff's Amnesia**

   - individuals who chronically consume alcohol develop a pattern of behavioral disorders commonly referred to as **Korsakoff's syndrome**
   - in addition to severe **anterograde amnesia**, Korsakoff patients suffer from a severe **retrograde amnesia**
   - although their retrograde amnesia is more severe for recent memories, it also affects their memory for events occurring many years before the diagnosis of their case (i.e., for remote events); this temporal gradient is usually assumed to reflect a gradient of retrograde amnesia, however, it could reflect the insidious development of anterograde deficits prior to diagnosis--or a combination of both
   - Korsakoff patients display near normal implicit memory but show severe deficits in explicit memory
   - **repetition priming tasks** are used to test implicit memory; in a word version of the task subjects examine a list of words and later are presented with fragments of words from the list; when asked to complete the fragments with the first words that come to mind amnesics with damage to the medial temporal lobe or the medial diencephalon (such as patients with Korsakoff's) typically complete the word fragments using list words; their performance is similar to normal subjects but they have **no explicit memory** for the list or for having seen it before
   - the brain damage associated with Korsakoff's amnesia is diffuse, but the amnesia is usually attributed to medial diencephalic damage, particularly to the **mediodorsal nuclei of the thalamus**
   - Korsakoff patients also have damage to **prefrontal cortex**; like patients with damage restricted to prefrontal cortex, they do not display deficits in **memory for temporal sequence**

4. **The Case of N.A.**

   - after his junior year in college, N.A. joined the airforce; one day in the barracks, he was accidentally stabbed in the brain through the right nostril by a friend with a fencing foil; he suffered both retrograde and anterograde amnesia
   - the foil penetrated the **cribriform plate; a** subsequent MRI revealed extensive damage in medial diencephalon, including the **mediodorsal nuclei** and the **mammillary bodies**
   - although it did not show up on the CAT scan test, there must have been damage to structures other than the mediodorsal nucleus; but N.A.'s case is consistent with the view that the mediodorsal nucleus is important in memory
   - unlike Korsakoff patients, N.A. shows normal memory for **temporal order**, which is consistent with the idea that the deficits in these abilities in Korsakoff patients result from their prefrontal cortex damage

5. **Memory Deficits and Prefrontal Cortex Damage**

   - damage to the prefrontal cortex produces two distinctive kinds of memory deficits: 1) Difficulty in Remembering the **Sequence of Events**; and 2) difficulty in performing **self-ordered tasks**, in which a person has to remember which of a sequence of actions they have already performed and which actions must still be performed to complete a task.

6. **Alzheimer's Disease**

   - this is the most common cause of **dementia** affecting almost 5% of people over the age of 65; it begins with mild amnesia and results in terminal dysfunction
   - pathological changes include **neurofibrillary tangles** (in neural cytoplasm), **amyloid plaques**(scar tissue in degenerating neurons), and **reductions in neurotransmitters**, especially **acetylcholine**; these changes are widespread, but most predominant in **temporal, frontal,** and the **parietal cortex**
   - **nootropics** are drugs that enhance memory; several different drugs have been used in Alzheimer's patients, with mixed success

7. **Posttraumatic Amnesia** *(use Digital Image Archive Figure CH14F08.BMP)*

   - blows to the head can lead to posttraumatic amnesia including a loss of consciousness (**coma**), periods of confusion, and a permanent retrograde amnesia (for events preceding the blow); such deficits are also seen following **electroconvulsive shock** treatments

106

Suggested Websites for Lecture 14a:

Alzheimer's Disease: *http://www.med.harvard.edu/publications/On_The_Brain/Volume2/Special/SPAlz.html*

From Harvard University's Mahoney Neuroscience Institute, a dialogue on aging and Alzheimer's Disease led by Dr. Marilyn Albert and Dr. Huntington Potter. See also:

http://www.alzheimers.org/

for the home page of the Alzheimer's Disease page of the National Institute on Aging.

The Hippocampus: *http://thalamus.wustl.edu/course/limbic.html*

From Washington University's Neuroscience tutorial; see the second half of this page for some great anatomical figures (including effects of hypoxia on the CA1 cells of the hippocampal formation) and text discussing the role of the hippocampus in memory.

Prefrontal Cortex: *http://www.sciam.com/0897issue/0897trends.html*

From Scientific American, an overview of the role of the prefrontal cortex in memory function; good figures and links to other sites.

Concussions: *http://www.miaims.missouri.edu/~neuromedicine/concussion.shtml*

From the University of Missouri's Health Sciences Center, a review of the causes and signs of concussion.

Lecture 14b

ANIMAL MODELS IN THE STUDY OF
BRAIN-DAMAGE-PRODUCED AMNESIA

Outline

1. Inadequacy of Early Animal Models of Amnesia

2. A New Paradigm to Assess Memory in Animals: Nonrecurring-Items Delayed Nonmatching-to-Sample
   a. Monkeys
   b. Rats

3. The Use of Animal Models to Study the Neural Bases of Memory
   a. Which Structures Contribute to Medial-Temporal-Lobe Amnesia?
   b. The Hippocampus and Memory for Spatial Location

4. Review of Brain Areas Contributing to Memory

5. Conclusion

Lecture Notes

1. **Inadequacy of Early Animal Models of Amnesia**

   - animal models allow for the controlled experiments needed to answer questions about the neural bases of memory and amnesia; human subjects are precluded from experimental lesioning and other methods required for research; however, human clinical case studies complement animal research
   - it was first believed that H.M. could not form any type of long-term memories; as a result, attempts to duplicate the amnesic effects of bilateral medial-temporal-lobe lesions in animals paid little attention to the type of retention tests that were employed
   - these early attempts were unsuccessful; in retrospect it is apparent that they focused on the kind of tests on which H.M. himself showed no deficits (tests of **implicit memory**)

2. **A New Paradigm to Assess Memory in Animals: Nonrecurring-Items Delayed Nonmatching-to-Sample**

   - the task that has been used frequently to assess amnesia for objects in laboratory animals is the **nonrecurring-items delayed nonmatching-to-sample task**
   - the first and the most widely used version of this task was developed to assess amnesia in brain-damaged monkeys, but it has also been used to assess the amnesia of brain-damaged rats and humans

   a. Monkeys *(use Digital Image Archive Figure CH14F11.BMP)*

   - on each trial, the monkey must remember the <u>sample</u> object so that it can obtain the food from beneath the <u>nonsample</u> object on the test portion of the trial; different objects are used on each trial

108

b. **Rats** *(use Digital Image Archive Figure CH14F17.BMP)*
- Mumby and Pinel (1990) developed a version of the nonmatching-to-sample paradigm for rats; remarkably, the performance of rats is not substantially different from that of monkeys at retention intervals of up to 5 minutes
- the rat runs to one end of a straight alley and pushes the sample object aside to get a morsel of food; the sample is removed and the rat is kept in that end by an opaque door until the appropriate delay has passed; the door is then raised and the animal must run to the two objects at the other end and push aside the nonsample to obtain the morsel beneath it; then the rat is in a position to begin the next trial without having to be removed from the **Mumby box** *(use Digital Image Archive Figure CH14F15.BMP)*

3. **The Use of Animal Models to Study the Neural Bases of Memory**

a. **Which Structures Contribute to Medial-Temporal-Lobe Amnesia?**

- medial temporal lobectomy damages several major neural structures; initially it was concluded that the amnesia resulted from hippocampal damage because there seemed to be a correlation between the amount of hippocampal damage and the amount of amnesia in the few patients that had been studied
- however, it is difficult to answer this question with confidence based on the incomplete and unsystematic data collected from human patients; the development of the monkey model provided a complementary means of approaching this question
- one alternative to Milner's original **hippocampus hypothesis** is the **hippocampus-plus-amygdala hypothesis** in which severe amnesia does not occur unless both the amygdala and hippocampus are damaged
- recent findings favor another hypothesis. They are based on the observaton that because hippocampal and amygdalar lesions in humans and monkeys are usually made by aspiration, the medial-temporal cortex (**entorhinal, perirhinal,** and **perihippocampal cortex**) that overlies them is usually also removed
- the importance of this observation emerged when it was demonstrated in both monkeys (Meunier et al., 1990; Zola-Morgan et al., 1989) and rats (Mumby et al., 1989) that lesions of the hippocampus that do not damage overlying cortex produce only mild deficits in nonrecurring-items delayed nonmatching-to-sample tests; furthermore, lesions of medial-temporal cortex that do not damage the hippocampus produce major deficits
- these data cast into doubt the conclusions reached based on the ischemic patient R.B., who displayed amnesia attributed to damage to the CA1 cell subfield of the hippocampus. In a recent experiment, Mumby and his colleagues showed that ischemia-induced amnesia in the nonrecurring-items delayed nonmatching-to-sample tests in rats can be *blocked* by large bilateral hippocampectomy...suggesting that the hippocampal damage displayed by R.B. did not contribute significantly to his amnesia!

b. **Hippocampus and Memory for Spatial Location**

- although the hippocampus may not be critical to the performance of the nonrecurring-items delayed nonmatching-to-sample test, it does appear to be involved in the mediation of spatial memory
- two techniques are widely used to test spatial memory

    1) the **Morris water maze test** requires rats to learn the location of an invisible stationary platform and find it when swimming in opaque (usually milk-white) water; rats with hippocampal lesions have great difficulty with this task whereas control rats without hippocampal damage easily learn the task

    2) in the **radial arm maze test,** there is a central chamber with as many as 8 alleys or "arms" radiating from it. During each test, a few of the 8 arms of the apparatus are baited with some kind of reward; intact rats learn to visit only the baited arms (this is referred to as **reference memory**); rats with hippocampal lesions show deficits in reference memory in that they do not

exclusively visit baited arms. In addition, they show deficits in **working memory** as they repeatedly visit unbaited arms during each test

- further evidence for the role of the hippocampus in spatial memory comes from the existence of hippocampal **place cells**, first identified in rats by O'Keefe and Dostrovsky (1971); these cells fired when a rat is placed in a specific location, but only after becoming familiar with that location
- in addition, Sherry and his colleagues (1992) have reported that food caching birds birds tend to have larger hippocampi than noncaching species

4. **Review of Brain Areas Contributing to Memory** *(use Digital Image Archive Figure CH14F19.BMP)*

- **Rhinal cortex**: major role in the formation of long term memory for objects
- **Hippocampus:** consolidation of long term memories for spatial location
- **Amygdala:** memory for the emotional significance of experience
- **Inferotemporal cortex:** storage of long-term visual memories
- **Cerebellum and Striatum:** implicit sensorimotor memory
- **Prefrontal cortex**: memory for temporal order of events; possible role in the retrieval of memories
- **Mediodorsal nucleus:** damage leads to memory deficits; the medial diencephalic and medial temporal lobes may be in the same memory circuit
- **Basal forebrain:** serve a variety of functions with a controversial role in memory

5. **Conclusion**

- the study of brain-damage-produced amnesia illustrates the inferential power of **converging operations**
- controlled animal experiments, clinical case studies, and quasiexperimental studies on groups of human patients have complemented one another
- together they have greatly improved our understanding of the neural bases of amnesia; these gains would not have been possible with one approach alone; this is a very active area of research and one gets the impression that major breakthroughs will soon be forthcoming

Suggested Websites for Lecture 14b:

The Hippocampus: *http://thalamus.wustl.edu/course/limbic.html*

From Washington University's Neuroscience tutorial; see the second half of this page for some great anatomical figures (including effects of hypoxia on the CA1 cells of the hippocampal formation) and text discussing the role of the hippocampus in memory. See also:

http://psy.otago.ac.nz:800/eric/seahorse.htm

for an excellent reference on the hippocampal formation and its role in memory.

Prefrontal Cortex: *http://www.sciam.com/0897issue/0897trends.html*

From Scientific American, an overview of the role of the prefrontal cortex in memory function; good figures and links to other sites.

Tests of Memory: *http://olias.arc.nasa.gov/cognition/tutorials/index.html*

From NASA's Ames Research Center, five tests of memory function...have fun!

Lecture 15a

NEURAL DEVELOPMENT

Outline

1. Induction of the Neural Plate

2. Neural Proliferation

3. Migration and Aggregation

4. Axon Growth and the Formation of Synapses
   a. Chemoaffinity Hypothesis
   b. Blueprint Hypothesis
   c. Topographic-Gradient Hypothesis

5. Neural Death and Synapse Rearrangement

6. Effects of Experience on Neural Development

Lecture Notes

- each product of sexual reproduction begins life as a single cell (**zygote**)
- during the development of the **embryo**, the first observable step in the development of the nervous system is the induction of the **neural plate**

1. **Induction of the Neural Plate** *(use Digital Image Archive Figure CH15F01.BMP)*

   - about 3 weeks after conception, a patch of **ectoderm** on the dorsal surface of the embryo becomes distinguishable from the rest of the ectoderm; this patch is the neural plate, and it eventually develops into the nervous system
   - prior to induction of the neural plate, the cells of the dorsal ectoderm are **totipotential** (that is, if they are transplanted to a new site in the embryo, they develop in the same way as cells at the new site); after neural plate induction, they develop into nervous system cells even if they are transplanted to another site in the embryo
   - the differentiation of the cells of the neural plate seems to be **induced** by the underlying **mesoderm** in one experiment, a piece of mouse mouth mesoderm was implanted next to the ectoderm of a chick embryo, and recognizable teeth were induced to develop from the chick ectoderm
   - the neural plate develops into the **neural groove** and then into the **neural tube**, which subsequently develops into the CNS
   - some cells break off from the neural plate and form the **neural crest**, which lies dorsal to the neural tube and subsequently develops into the PNS

2. **Neural Proliferation**

   - after the neural tube is formed, the developing nervous system cells rapidly increase in number
   - three bulges appear at the anterior end of the neural tube and become the **forebrain, midbrain** and **hindbrain**
   - cell division occurs in the **ventricular zone** of the neural tube (the zone next to the ventricle); when they leave the cell division cycle, cells migrate into other layers

3. **Migration and Aggregation** *(use Digital Image Archive Figure CH15F03.BMP)*

- cells migrate away from the ventricular zone along a temporary network of **radial glial cells**, which are present in only the developing neural tube
- the cells of the neocortex migrate in an **inside-out pattern**; the deepest layers form first so that the cells of the superficial layers must migrate through them
- migration of the cells of the neural crest is of particular interest because these cells ultimately form the PNS, and thus many have a long way to migrate
- neural crest cells transplanted to a new part of the neural crest migrate to the destination that is appropriate for cells in the new location; thus the migration routes must be encoded in the medium rather than in the cells; **differential adhesion** to routes through the medium is hypothesized to guide the migration of future PNS neurons
- once migration is complete, cells must **aggregate** correctly to form various neural structures; this is hypothesized to be mediated by specialized neural cell **adhesion molecules** in the cell membranes (NCAMs)

4. **Axon Growth and the Formation of Synapses**

- once the aggregation of developing neurons is complete, axons and dendrites grow out from the neurons; growing to the correct target is particularly difficult for axons that have a long way to grow
- studies in which the same recognizable developing neuron has been labeled in different subjects demonstrate that the axons of some particular neurons grow to the same destination by the same route in every member of a species; this accurate axon growth seems to be directed by a **growth cone** at the growing axon tip
- three hypotheses have been proposed to explain how growth cones make their way to their correct destination: (1) the **chemoaffinity hypothesis**, (2) the **blueprint hypothesis**, and (3) the **topographic-gradient hypothesis**
- axon growth is often studied in **regenerating** neurons; it is assumed that axonal growth and regrowth are guided by the same mechanisms

   a. **Chemoaffinity Hypothesis**
   - Sperry's classic eye-rotation regeneration experiments remain the classic example of data supporting the chemoaffinity hypothesis *(use Digital Image Archive Figure CH15F05.BMP)*
   - Sperry cut the optic nerves of frogs, rotated their eyes, and waited for regeneration; after regeneration, it was clear from their misdirected feeding responses that the visual world of the frogs was rotated by the same degree as the eye rotation, the axons seemed to have regenerated back to their original targets
   - on the basis of this series of studies, Sperry proposed the chemoaffinity hypothesis; the hypothesis that the target of each growing axon has a specific chemical label that draws the correct growing axon to it
   - but the chemoaffinity hypothesis can't explain why some neurons grow to their correct targets via indirect routes, and it can't explain why a target structure transplanted to an unnatural site becomes incorrectly innervated; when Whitelaw & Hollyday (1983) transplanted an extra thigh segment onto the leg of a developing chick embryo (so that it looked like a thigh, transplanted thigh, calf, foot…wonder what poultry growers would say about that!), it became innervated by neurons that would normally have innervated the calf

   b. **Blueprint hypothesis**
   - another problem with the chemoaffinity hypothesis is that it cannot explain how some developing axons follow the same indirect route in every member of a species
   - the **blueprint hypothesis** (the hypothesis that the substrate contains physical and chemical trails that growth cones follow to their correct destinations) was proposed to account for the accuracy of axon growth
   - only the first axon that grows into an area must have the ability to reach its correct target; the others appear to follow the **pioneer growth cone's** route by a process called **fasciculation** if a pioneer axon growth cone is destroyed by a laser, few of the other neurons in the nerve reach their correct destinations.

- but the blueprint hypothesis cannot explain how some developing axons manage to grow to their correct targets even when their starting points have been surgically shifted. For example, Lance-Jones and Landmesser (1980) cut out a piece of the spinal cord of a chick embryo, inverted it, and reimplanted it; nevertheless, the axons grew out to their correct targets *(use Digital Image Archive Figure CH15F06.BMP)*

   c. **Topographic-Gradient Hypothesis**
- the **topographic-gradient hypothesis** is that axon growth from one topographic array (such as a retina) is guided by the relative position of the cell bodies and terminals on two intersecting gradients
- the topographic-gradient hypothesis is supported by the fact that lesions of part of optic tectum cause optic nerve axons that have been transected to grow out to fill the available space in relation to their position on a two-dimensional topographic map of the retina, regardless of how much tectum is left. Similarly, lesions of the part of the retina cause regenerating axons to fill the optic tectum in a way that matches the topography of the remaining retina *(use Digital Image Archive Figure CH15F07.BMP)*

Summary: all the evidence on axon growth and regeneration suggests that a variety of mechanisms can guide axon growth; the growth of different axons appears to be guided by different combinations of these mechanisms

5. Neuron Death and Synapse Rearrangement

- up to 50% of neurons that develop die shortly thereafter; the fact that neurons that make incorrect connections are more likely to die suggests that cell death increases the overall accuracy of synaptic connections
- three lines of evidence suggest that neurons die because they fail to compete successfully for some life-preserving factor (neurotropins such as **nerve growth factor**) supplied by their target:

  (1) implantation of an extra target site decreases neuron death (e.g., an implanted extra limb decreases motor neuron loss);
  (2) destroying some neurons before the period of neuron death increases the survival rate of the remainder; and
  (3) increasing the number of axons that initially synapse on a target decreases survival rate of the remainder

- most of this cell death is due to **apoptosis;** preprogrammed cell death that is believed to result from the lack of an appropriate trophic factor.
- in addition, there is **synapse rearrangement** during an organism's lifespan; its effect is to focus the output of each neuron on fewer postsynaptic neurons *(use Digital Image Archive Figure CH15F08.BMP)*

6. Effects of Experience on Neural Development

- neuroplasticity reflects the changes in the mature nervous system that underlie learning: **"use it or lose it"** applies here as neurons and synapses that are not active do not survive
- researchers have found fewer dendritic spines in visual cortex areas when organisms were deprived of vision, and increases in synapses and dendrites when animals were placed in visually enriched environments
- in a graphic example of the competition that underlies synapse rearrangement, Lo and Poo (1991) demonstrated *in vitro* that stimulating one of two motor neurons that innervated the same muscle cell caused a rapid degradation of synaptic contacts between the other, inactive motor neuron and the cell
- in a similar vein, Hubel, Wiesel, and LeVay (1977) showed that early monocular deprivation, reduces the width of the deprived eye's ocular dominance stripes in layer IV
- experience alters neural development in at least 3 different ways: 1) by influencing **gene expression**; 2) by influencing the release of **neurotrophins**; and 3) by influencing the release of **neurotransmitters** like norepinephrine that play a role in normal development.

Suggest Websites for Lecture 15a:

Brain Development...Genetics and Environment: *http://www.real.com/rafiles/npr/nf6f0901.ram*

From National Public Radio, an audio examination of the role of genes and experience on brain development; includes commentary by Dr. Marian Diamond, Dr. Joanne Berger-Sweeney, Dr. Mary Blue, and Dr. Craig Ramey. See also:

http://weber.u.washington.edu/~chudler/dev.html

Another excellent page from Dr. Eric Chudler at the University of Washington; good text and figures, and many good links to other relevant websites.

Growth Cones: *http://gramercy.ios.com/%7Epab9/*

A neat site presenting several B&W movies of the growth cones of retinal ganglion cells, accompanied by explanatory text. Download their movie viewer if yours will not support .MOV format files.

Degeneration, Regeneration, and Reorganization: *http://www.hhmi.org/senses/e/e210.htm*

From the Howard Hughes Medical Center, an article describing the reorganization of a person's somatosensory homunculus after surgery. Brief but interesting.

Lecture 15b

LEARNING IN SIMPLE SYSTEMS

Outline

1. The Simple-Systems Approach to the Study of Learning

2. The *Aplysia* Gill-Withdrawal-Reflex Circuit

3. Mechanisms of Memory in *Aplysia*
   a. Nonassociative Learning
   b. Associative Learning
   c. Second Messengers and Structural Changes in *Aplysia* Conditioning

4. Long-Term Potentiation

5. Conclusion

Lecture Notes

1. The **Simple-Systems Approach** to the Study of Learning:

   - it is an approach that focuses on the most simple forms of learning in the most simple circuits that can mediate them
   - researchers who take this approach believe that studying simple forms of learning in simple circuits is likely to reveal the fundamental principles of the neural basis of learning in complex systems and that these principles would not be discovered by studying complex systems directly
   - **learning** refers to the induction of experience produced neural changes
   - **memory** refers to the maintenance of the "learned" neural changes and later use of them in the form of behavioral changes

2. The *Aplysia* **Gill-Withdrawal Reflex Circuit**

   - *Aplysia* is a simple marine snail; it spends its life oozing along the ocean floor eating seaweed and expelling excess sea water and waste through a small fleshy spout called a **siphon** *(use Digital Image Archive Figure CH15F10.BMP)*
   - if the siphon is touched, the siphon and gill of the *Aplysia* are immediately drawn up under a protective **mantle**; this is the *Aplysia* gill-withdrawal reflex *(use Digital Image Archive Figure CH15F11.BMP)*
   - the *Aplysia* gill-withdrawal reflex is mediated by 24 sensory neurons in the skin of the siphon, a few small interneurons, and 6 motor neurons that are responsible for gill and siphon retraction

3. **Mechanisms of Memory in *Aplysia***

   a. **Nonassociative Learning in *Aplysia***
      - forms of nonassociative learning include learning that does not involve the learning of relations; nonassociative learning results from the single presentation of a stimulus, the repeated presentation of the same stimulus, or the presentation of two or more unrelated stimuli
      - habituation and sensitization are two kinds of nonassociative learning that have been studied in the *Aplysia* gill-withdrawal reflex circuit

1. **Habituation** *(use Digital Image Archive Figure CH15F12A.BMP)*
   - **habituation** is the **decrease** in the strength of the behavioral reaction to a stimulus following repeated presentation of the stimulus
   - habituation of the *Aplysia* gill-withdrawal reflex lasts 2 or 3 hours after one 10-stimulation session, but a series of many habituation sessions can produce habituation that lasts for weeks
   - habituation was found to be associated with a decline in the number of action potentials in the gill motor neurons; this decrease in activity was due to a **decrease in the amount of neurotransmitter released** by the sensory neuron terminals in response to their own action potentials
   - the decrease in neurotransmitter released with each action potential by the sensory neurons was found to be due to a decrease in the number of **Ca++ ions** entering the terminal buttons of sensory neurons during repeated stimuli, and to a **depletion on neurotransmitter pools** in the sensory axon terminals

2. **Sensitization** *(use Digital Image Archive Figure CH15F12B.BMP)*

   - in contrast to habituation, **sensitization** is an **increase** in the strength of a response;
   - in *Aplysia*, one severe electric shock to the tail will increase the amplitude of the gill-withdrawal reflex lasts several minutes; following a series of tail shocks over several days, sensitization can last for weeks
   - in contrast to habituation, sensitization results from an **increase in the amount of neurotransmitter released** by the siphon sensory neuron terminals in response to each of their own action potentials; this increase is brought about by **presynaptic facilitation** from interneurons
   - interneurons show an increased influx of Ca++ ions into terminal buttons
   - the increased Ca++ leads to more neurotransmitter released from the interneuron onto motor neurons, and the motor neurons' firing is thus enhanced
   - there is also some evidence that the motor neurons themselves also increase their excitability

b. **Associative Learning in *Aplysia*** *(use Digital Image Archive Figure CH15F13.BMP)*

   - in **associative learning**, subjects learn the relation between stimuli, or between stimuli and responses
   - the *Aplysia* gill-withdrawal reflex circuit is capable of Pavlovian conditioning; in experiments on Pavlovian conditioning in *Aplysia*, the **conditional stimulus** (CS) has been a touch to the siphon, which is too light to elicit much gill withdrawal; the **unconditional stimulus** (US) has been a tail shock, which always elicits strong gill withdrawal (the **unconditional response** or UR); after several pairings of light siphon touch and tail shock, the light siphon touch elicits a strong gill withdrawal (which is the **conditioned response** or CR).
   - the strongest evidence of the associative nature of this phenomena comes from studies of discriminated conditioning; in which a CS+ (a conditional stimulus paired with the US during the conditioning trials) comes to elicit a CR while a CS- (a conditional stimulus that is never paired with the US) does not
   - Pavlovian conditioning of the *Aplysia* gill withdrawal reflex can be thought of as a special case of sensitization; it is simply an instance of sensitization in which the sensitizing effect of tail shock is greatest on those reflexes elicited by stimuli that were presented just prior to each of a series of shocks
   - this is thought to occur because the tail shock activates interneurons that have a excitatory effect on the presynaptic terminal buttons of sensory neurons that were active just before the tail shock; this is called **activity-dependent** synaptic facilitation *(use Digital Image Archive Figure CH15F14.BMP)*

c. **Second Messengers and Structural Changes in *Aplysia* Conditioning**

   - Byrne et al., (1993) and Krasne and Glanzman (1995) have implicated **second messengers** in long-term memory storage during *Aplysia* conditioning
   - second messengers are created inside postsynaptic neurons in response to a neurotransmitter binding to a G-protein linked receptor
   - **Cyclic AMP** is a second messenger generated by *Aplysia* during sensitization; it activates **protein kinase C,** which closes potassium channels in the terminal buttons of siphon sensory neurons, thus

increasing the duration of each action potential allowing greater influx of calcium and more neurotransmitter released in response to each touch of the siphon
- long-term memory storage in *Aplysia* requires second messengers capable of stimulating protein synthesis in neuron cell bodies; Bailey and Chen (1988) have reported that long-term habituation induces decreases in the size of presynaptic active zones and in the number of **synaptic vesicles** in the terminal buttons of sensory neurons, whereas sensitization induces the opposite types of changes.

4. Long-Term Potentiation

- the simple-systems approach does not always focus on simple organisms; sometimes it focuses on simple components of neural circuits in complex organisms; for example, **long-term potentiation** (LTP) has been studied at a variety of synapses in the mammalian central nervous system
- in an LTP experiment, a brief period of **intense high-frequency stimulation** enhances the subsequent repsonse of postsynaptic neurons to low-intensity stimulation of the presynaptic neurons. This enhancement can last for weeks depending on the number, duration, frequency, and intensity of the inducing stimulations
- LTP is often studied in the **hippocampal-slice preparation** *(use Digital Image Archive Figure CH15F15.BMP);* for example, LTP has frequently been studied in terms of changes in the response of neurons in the **granule-cell layer** of the **hippocampal dentate gyrus** following intense high-frequency **perforant path** stimulation *(use Digital Image Archive Figure CH15F16.BMP)*
- LTP is interesting because it is the kind of change that was postulated by Hebb in 1949 to underlie memory; Hebb suggested that such changes would be reasonably permanent (which LTP is) and that such synaptic facilitation would occur only when both the presynaptic and the postsynaptic neurons were simultaneously active. This need for **cooccurrence** of activation is called **Hebb's postulate for learning**; it has been demonstrated that **co-occurrence** of activity in presynaptic and postsynaptic neurons is necessary for LTP
- the **NMDA** (N-methyl-D-aspartate) **glutamate** receptor appears to mediate hippocampal LTP; for example, drugs that block the NMDA subtype of glutamate receptors block the LTP produced by perforant path stimulation without blocking synaptic transmission itself; furthermore, NMDA-mediated activation of postsynaptic neurons requires that the postsynaptic cell already be depolarized by concurrent activation by nonNMDA receptors; this requirement for cooccurrence of activity is an important feature of LTP and its putative relationship to learning mechanisms *(use Digital Image Archive Figure CH15F18.BMP)*
- it is unclear whether maintenance and expression of LTP are due to presynaptic or postsynaptic changes; however some research has offered clues:

    1) Harris & Kater (1994) have found that the specificity of LTP to specific presynaptic inputs is attributable to calcium entering only those **dendritic spines** that are activated during the high-frequency stimulation.
    2) Nguyen, Abel & Kandell (1994) have found that **blocking protein synthesis** immediately after the administration of high-frequency stimulation has no effect on the maintenance of LTP for one or two hours, but blocks its maintenance for longer periods
    3) Several researchers have suggested that **nitric oxide** (NO), a soluble gas neurotransmitter, may serve as the signal that passes from the postsynaptic neuron back to the presynaptic neuron to induce and maintain LTP. NO is produced by the postsynaptic cell during high-frequency stimulation, and NO inhibitors block long-term maintenance of LTP.

5. Conclusion

- research on both LTP and conditioning of the *Aplysia* gill-withdrawal reflex suggests that synaptic facilitation is capable of storing experiences for relatively long periods of time (as Hebb proposed in 1949)
- whether or not similar but more elaborate mechanisms mediate more complex forms of learning and memory (such as learning and remembering the contents of this lecture!) remains to be demonstrated

Suggested Websites for Lecture 15b:

Aplysia Hometank: *http://ganglion.med.cornell.edu/Hometank.html*

From Cornell University, everything you ever needed to know about recording from the favourite mollusc of brain scientists...after escargot, of course! See also:

http://nba19.uth.tmc.edu/nrc/newsltr/winter95/nrcnews1.html

for a review of work on Aplysia and learning and memory.

Long Term Potentiation: *http://psy.otago.ac.nz:800/eric/ltp.htm*

From Eric Hargreave at the University of Otago, a developing page giving a good overview of the phenomenon of long-term potentiation.

http://www.the-scientist.library.upenn.edu/yr1999/mar/russo_p1_990301.html

From *The Scientist,* an interesting and balanced look at the controversy surrounding the putative relationship between long term potentiaon and memory. For a more biased view, but one that is very intersting as well, see:

ftp://ftp.princeton.edu/pub/harnad/BBS/.WWW/bbs.shors.html

for a preprint of Shors and Matzel's article in Behavioral and Brain Sciences entitled *"Long-Term Potentiation: What's Learning Got to Do With It?"*.

Lecture 15c

DEGENERATION, REGENERATION, NEUROTRANSPLANTATION AND RECOVERY OF FUNCTION IN THE NERVOUS SYSTEM

Outline

1. Neural Damage: Degeneration, Regeneration, and Reorganization
   a. Degeneration
   b. Regeneration
   c. Reorganization

2. Therapeutic Implications of Neuroplasticity
   a) Promotion of Recovery by Rehabilitative Training
   b) Promotion of Recovery by Genetic Engineering
   c) Promotion of Recovery by Neurotransplantation

Lecture Notes

1. **Neural Damage: Degeneration, Regeneration, and Reorganization**

   a. **Degeneration:** *(use Digital Image Archive Figure CH15F19.BMP)*

   - is a deterioration of the neuron following damage. There are 2 main types:

      1) **anterograde degeneration** involves **distal segments** of the axon and occurs rapidly following an axotomy; the entire segment of the axon that was separated from the cell body swells and within a few days breaks into fragments.

      2) **retrograde degeneration** includes changes in the axon from   the site of damage back to the soma over a 2-3 day period; if early changes show an increase in the size, the neuron will likely regenerate the axon; if early changes include a decrease in size the cell will probably degenerate and die

   - **phagocytosis** is a cleaning of debris after damage; in the CNS this is performed by astroglia and in the PNS the Schwann cells (which compose the myelin sheaths) perform the task
   - **transneuronal degeneration** is the spread of degeneration from damaged neurons to neurons on which they synapse; **anterograde transneuronal degeneration** is when neurons postsynaptic to the damaged cell are affected; **retrograde transneuronal degeneration** is when cells, presynaptic to the damaged cell are affected

   b. **Regeneration:** *(use Digital Image Archive Figure CH15F20.BMP)*

   - is a regrowth of the damaged neurons; this occurs more readily in invertebrates than in higher vertebrate; it is almost nonexistent in the CNS and at best a "hit or miss" affair in adult mammals
   - in mammalian PNS regeneration, regrowth from the proximal stump of the damaged neuron begins 2-3 days after damage; if the myelin sheath is intact, regrowth may be guided through the myelin sheath and toward the original   target; however, if a segment of the nerve has been cut the regenerating axons may grow into incorrect sheaths and thus to incorrect targets; the axon may grow in a tangled mass without direction
   - **collateral sprouting** is the growth of axon branches from adjacent healthy neurons and may occur at the site of degenerating neurons *(use Digital Image Archive Figure CH15F21.BMP)*

c. __Reorganization__ *(use Digital Image Archive Figure CH15F22.BMP)*

- damage to sensory and motor pathways, the sensory and motor cortexes, and distortion of sensory experiences have all been used to study neural reorganization in adult mammals
- for example, Kaas et al., (1990) found that retinal lesions resulted in __new visual receptive fields__ being developed in the primary visual cortex that had originally received input from the lesioned areas of retina. These changes began within minutes of the retinal lesion.
- in an experiment employing altered sensory inputs, Recanzone et al., (1992) found that exposing primates to sensory stimuli on the third digit, resulted in an __expansion of the representation__ of that digit in primary somatosensory cortex.
- Sanes, Suner & Donoghue (1990) found that transection of rat motor neurons that controlled the vibrassae muscles resulted in the associated motor cortex areas activating other parts of the face after a few weeks *(use Digital Image Archive Figure CH15F22.BMP)*
- __the reorganization of neural connections is believed to occur via 2 types of changes:__ *(use Digital Image Archive Figure CH15F23.BMP)*

    1) rapid reorganization of neural connections usually results from experience; this is believed to reflect the strengthening of existing connections; and

    2) gradual reorganization usually results from neural damage; this is believed to reflect the establishment of new connections via collateral sprouting.

- although the actual extent of neural reorganization and recovery of function after brain damage remains controversial, 3 general conclusions have emerged: 1) bona fide recovery of function is rare; 2) small lesions are more likely to be associated with recovery of function than large lesions; and 3) recovery of function is more likely in young patients.

2. __Therapeutic Implications of Neuroplasticity__

a) __Promotion of Recovery by Rehabilitative Training__:

- small strokes often produce a core of damage, which is followed by a gradually expanding loss of function around this core. This latter loss can be reduced in motor cortex by __rehabilitative training__.
- for example, recovery of function following damage to the had area of motor cortex in primates is facilitated if the monkeys engage in manual tasks during their recuperation; there is less loss of tissue and greater recovery of manual dexterity.
- following spinal cord injury in humans, people receiving rehabilitative training showed greater recovery of function (walking) than people that simply received conventional physiotherapy.

b) __Promotion of Recovery by Genetic Engineering__:

- key idea is to increase __neurotrophin__ levels to promote regeneration; this can be done by introducing genetically-altered stem cells that produce neurotrophin into the damaged nervous system, or by injecting genetically altered viruses that will promote neurotrophin production by host cells into the damaged nervous system.

c) __Promotion of Recovery by Neurotransplantation__:

- rat brain tissue was first transplanted successfully in the early 1970's (Das & Altman, 1971)
- subsequent research shows that __conspecific__ brain tissue transplant rejections are rare, especially if the transplanted tissues are from __fetal donors__

- the objective of most transplant research is to develop techniques to treat CNS disorders by:

    (a) improving the function of the patient's own damaged tissue via regeneration, or
    (b) transplant cells that will integrate into the CNS and replace damaged tissue

- Aguayo and his colleagues have demonstrated the efficacy of the first approach; after cutting the **optic nerves** in rats, they introduced a piece of **sciatic nerve** that extended from the stump of the optic nerve to the **superior colliculus** *(use Digital Image Archive Figure CH15F26.BMP)*
- the regenerating axons from the **retinal ganglion cells** grew in the Schwann cell "tube" that was left as the axons of the sciatic nerve decayed; after 4 months they had grown back to the superior colliculus.
- using a similar technique, Cheng et al. (1996) subsequently showed that regenerated axons in the **spinal cord** were functional; rats that had been rendered **paraplegic** due to spinal cord damage regained the ability to move if a piece of peripheral nerve was used to bridge the site of damage and guide regenerating spinal axons to their targets.
- some of the most promising examples of recovery of function promoted by transplantation of foreign cells into the nervous system come from research in the area of Parkinson's disease. In both nonhuman primates that have been treated with MPTP, and in human patients suffereing from MPTP poisoning or Parkinson's disease, transplantation of **fetal dopaminergic substantia nigra cells** into the **striatum** has been shown to significantly reduce the **Parkinsonian symptoms**.

Suggested Websites for Lecture 15c:

Transplantation in the CNS: *http://neurosurgery.mgh.harvard.edu/oisacson.htm*

> From Harvard University's Mahoney Neuroscience Institute, a look at the use of transplantation in the treatment of Parkinson's Disease; complete with a mini-movie about the transplantation of porcine dopamine cells.

Neural Reorganization: *http://www.hhmi.org/senses/e/e210.htm*

> From the Howard Hughes Medical Center, an article describing the reorganization of a person's somatosensory homunculus after surgery. Brief but interesting.

Lecture 16a

LATERALIZATION AND THE SPLIT BRAIN

Outline

1. Aphasia and Apraxia: The Dominant Left Hemisphere

2. Tests of Language Laterality
   a. Sodium Amytal Test
   b. Dichotic Listening Test

3. Language Laterality and Handedness

4. The Ground-Breaking Split-Brain Experiment of Myers and Sperry

5. Tests of Split-Brain Patients
   a. Evidence of Two Independent Streams of Consciousness
   b. Cross Cuing
   c. Learning Two Things at Once
   d. Helping-Hand Phenomenon
   e. Comparing the Abilities of the Left and Right Hemispheres

6. Three Theories of Cerebral Asymmetry

Lecture Notes

1. Aphasia and Apraxia: The Dominant Left Hemisphere

- in 1836, **Dax**, an unknown country doctor, reported that not one of his 40 or so patients with speech problems had displayed damage restricted to the right hemisphere; his report attracted no interest
- 25 years later, **Broca** reported the results of the postmortem examination of two **aphasic** patients (patients with deficits in the use of language that are not attributable to general sensory, motor, or intellectual dysfunction); both had diffuse **left hemisphere damage** that seemed to be centered in an area of the inferior left prefrontal lobe, just in front of the primary motor face area *(use Digital Image Archive Figure CH16F02.BMP)*
- in the next few years, Broca examined 7 more brains of deceased aphasic patients; all had damage that included the same left frontal area, which became known as **Broca's area**
- subsequently, **Liepmann** discovered that **apraxia** (difficulty performing movements with either side of the body when asked to do so, but not when performing them spontaneously) was almost always associated with left hemisphere damage
- this led to the view that all complex activities were performed by the left hemisphere; the left and right hemispheres thus became known as the **dominant** and **minor** hemispheres, respectively

122

2. Tests of Language Laterality

- the first evidence of language laterality came from comparisons of the effects of left and right **unilateral lesions**; today, the **sodium amytal test** and the **dichotic listening test** are commonly used to assess language laterality

a. Sodium Amytal Test
- the sodium amytal test is administered to patients prior to neurosurgery so that the surgeon knows the side of speech lateralization and can take special care to avoid damaging the language areas; a small amount of **sodium amytal** is injected into one **carotid artery**, this anesthetizes the **ipsilateral** hemisphere and allows the abilities of the **contralateral** hemisphere to be assessed
- when the injection is made on the side of the dominant speech hemisphere (usually the left), the patient is totally **mute** for a minute or two, and as the ability to talk returns the patient makes speech errors (e.g., errors of naming and serial order); when the injection is on the side of the nondominant speech hemisphere (usually the right), there is no mutism and only a few speech errors

b. Dichotic Listening Test
- in the conventional form of the dichotic listening test, a sequence of three pairs of digits is presented through ear phones; the two digits of each pair are presented simultaneously, one digit to each ear
- when the subject is asked to report the 6 digits that she or he has heard, there is a slight but consistent tendency to report more of the digits presented to the ear contralateral to the dominant language hemisphere (usually the right ear)

3. Speech Laterality and Handedness

- many studies have reported a relation between speech laterality and handedness; the following general conclusions have been reached:

    (1) nearly all (about 95%) right-handed subjects are left-hemisphere dominant for speech;
    (2) most left-handed or ambidextrous subjects (about 70%) are also left-hemisphere dominant for speech; and
    (3) early left-hemisphere damage can cause the right hemisphere to become dominant for speech and the left hand to be preferred

4. The Ground-Breaking Split-Brain Experiment of Myers and Sperry

- in 1953, Myers and Sperry performed an experiment on cats that changed the way that we think about the brain; and it provided a means of comparing the functions of the two hemispheres; it was an experiment designed to reveal the function of the brain's largest **commissure**, the **corpus callosum**; the corpus callosum is the largest tract in the human brain, contains approximately 200 million axons, and it is the highest level at which the two cerebral hemispheres are connected *(use Digital Image Archive Figure CH16F01.BMP)*
- on the basis of its size and location, one would think that severing it would have devastating consequences; however, many earlier studies had failed to reveal any deficits in laboratory animals following **callosal transection**, and people born without a corpus callosum had been reported to be perfectly normal (leading some neuroscientists to joke that its job was to keep the cortex out of the ventricles!); Sperry was intrigued by the paradox
- in 1953, Myers and Sperry's published a groundbreaking paper that solved this apparent paradox. In their experiment, there were four groups of cats: (1) **corpus callosum** severed, (2) **optic chiasm** severed, (3) **corpus callosum and optic chiasm** severed, and (4) intact controls *(use Digital Image Archive Figure CH16F05.BMP)*
- in phase 1 of the experiment, all cats learned a lever-press pattern discrimination task with a **patch** over one eye; all four groups readily learned this simple task
- in phase 2, the patch was **switched** to the other eye; the cats in the optic-chiasm-severed group, in the corpus-callosum-severed group, and in the control group kept performing at close to 100% when the patch was shifted; in contrast, the cats with both their optic chiasms and corpus callosums severed, acted as if the task were completely new to them--they had to learn it again with no **savings**

- Meyers and Sperry concluded:: (1) the cat forebrain has the capacity to act as two separate forebrains, each capable of independent learning and of storing its own memories; (2) the function of the corpus callosum is to carry information between hemispheres; (3) the best strategy for studying corpus callosum function is to use a method to limit information to a single hemisphere (e.g., by cutting the optic chiasm and blindfolding one eye)

5. Tests of Split-Brain Patients

- **commissurotomy** is performed on patients with life-threatening cases of epilepsy to reduce the severity of convulsions by restricting epileptic discharges to half the brain
- the operation is remarkably effective; many commissurotomized epileptic patients never experience another major convulsion; more remarkably they experience few obvious side effects in their daily lives
- the controlled neuropsychological testing of these split-brain patients has revealed some amazing things about the human brain; the testing of the initial series of patients was conducted by Sperry and Gazzaniga
- to test split-brain patients, visual stimuli were flashed (to eliminate the effect of eye movement) on a screen to the left or right of a **fixation point** for **0.1 seconds** (contrast this method of limiting visual input to one hemisphere with the method used by Myers and Sperry in cats)
- tactual information was presented to one hand under a ledge or in a bag to prevent visual scanning of the objects; responses were either verbal responses or manual responses performed by one hand or the other under a ledge *(use Digital Image Archive Figure CH16F06.BMP)*
- amazingly, these tests confirmed the provocative conclusions of the experiments on split-brain laboratory animals in showing that the commissurotomized patients had **two independent streams of consciousness**; however, unlike split-brain laboratory animals the two hemispheres of commissurotomized patients were **not equal**; e.g., the left hemisphere could speak but the right could not

a. Evidence of Two Independent Streams of Consciousness
- when an object was presented to the **left hemisphere**, either by touching with the right hand or by viewing something in the right visual field, the subject could: (1) pick out the correct object with the right hand, (2) could not pick out the correct object with the left hand, (3) could name the correct object
- when an object was presented to the **right hemisphere**, either by touching with the left hand or by viewing something in the left visual field, the subject: (1) could pick out the correct object with the left hand, (2) could not pick out the correct object with the right hand, (3) claimed nothing had been presented
- if you are having difficulty understanding these results because you are used to thinking of yourself as an indivisible entity; think of each person as two subjects: (1) **Mr. or Ms. Right Hemisphere** who understands a few simple instructions but cannot speak, who receives sensory information from the left visual field and left hand, and who controls the fine motor responses of the left hand; and (2) **Mr. or Ms. Left Hemisphere** who understands complex speech and can speak, who receives sensory information from the right-visual field and right hand, and who controls the fine motor responses of the right hand
- if you find this a bit confusing imagine the confusion of the patient during the following test: An object was placed in the left hand of the patient, and the patient was asked what it was. The patient said (using her left hemisphere) that she couldn't tell. The experimenter berated the patient for not trying and suggested that she put the test object aside and try to pick out the correct object from an out-of-sight collection with her left hand (i.e., using her right hemisphere). Much to the patient's (the left hemisphere's) consternation, she did this correctly trial after trial, all the while claiming not to know the correct answer.

b. Cross-Cuing
- **cross-cuing** represents communication between hemispheres via a nonneural route
- for example, in one test, a red or a green light was flashed in the left visual field; the split-brain patient was then asked to name the color: red or green
- most split-brain patients get 50% correct on this task, however one patient eventually developed the ability to perform almost perfectly

- when the performance of this subject was carefully observed, it was noticed that on the trials when the patient initially said (the left hemisphere) the incorrect color, his head shook, and the patient then changed his guess to the other, correct color; apparently, the right hemisphere (who knew the correct answer) heard the incorrect guess of the left hemisphere, and signaled to the left hemisphere that it was wrong by shaking the person's head; when only first guesses were counted, performance immediately fell to 50%

c. **Learning Two Things at Once**
   - split-brain patients are capable of learning two things at once
   - if a split-brain patient is visually presented with two objects at the same time--let's say a pencil in the left visual field and an apple in the right--she or he can reach into two different bags at the same time, one with each hand, and pull out the two objects--a pencil in the left hand and an apple in the right
   - What would a split-brain subject say in this example if she were asked what she had in her hands before withdrawing them from the bags? ("two apples")

d. **Helping-Hand Phenomenon**
   - an interesting phenomenon, called the **helping-hand phenomenon**, occurs when the two hemispheres are presented with different information about the correct choice and then are asked to reach out and pick up the correct object from a collection in full view
   - usually the right hand will reach out to pick out what the left hemisphere saw (i.e., the apple in our previous example), but the right hemisphere seeing what it thinks is an error being made causes the left hand to grab the right hand and pull it over to the other object (i.e., the pencil in our previous example)

e. **Comparing the Abilities of the Left and Right Hemispheres**
   - split-brain patients provide neuropsychologists with an excellent opportunity to compare left and right hemisphere function; a device called a **Z lens** (after Zaidel) is used in many of these studies; it employs a contact lens that is opaque on one side to restrict visual input to one hemisphere, without being limited to 0.1-second presentations
   - not surprisingly, the left hemisphere proved better than the right at all **language-related tasks**; however, the right hemisphere proved to be able to understand written and spoken words and simple grammatical principles; the various language abilities of the right hemisphere proved to be comparable to those of a normal child between 3 and 6 years old
   - the left hemisphere has also proved to be better at controlling **ipsilateral body movements**
   - the right hemisphere proved better than the left at a variety of tasks, most notably those involving **spatial ability** (e.g., block designs subtest of the WAIS; **stereognosis**); it is also superior in processing **emotional stimuli** and for **musical tasks**
   - thus, the right hemisphere should not be regarded as the minor hemisphere; it has different abilities, not less important ones

6. **Three Theories of Cerebral Asymmetry**

   - Why has cerebral asymmetry evolved? Three main theories have tried to account for cerebral assymetry:

     1) According to the **Analytic-Synthetic Theory,** there are two fundamentally different modes of thinking, an **analytic mode** and a **synthetic mode**, and that the neural circuitry for each is fundamentally different; as a result, the two kinds of circuits are presumed to have become segregated during evolution, the analytic mode in the left hemisphere and the synthetic mode in the right
        - the left hemisphere, according to this theory, operates in a logical, sequential, analytic fashion; the right hemisphere makes immediate, overall synthetic judgments

     2) According to the **Motory Theory,** the left hemisphere is specialized for **fine motor movement** of which speech is but one example

- two lines of evidence support this theory: (1) lesions of the left hemisphere disrupt facial movements more than do right hemisphere lesions, even when they are not related to speech; (2) the degree of disruption of nonverbal facial movements is positively correlated with the degree of aphasia

3) According to the **Linguistic Theory**, the primary function of the left hemisphere is language; this is based on studies of deaf people who communicate using American Sign Language; this ability is lost if these people suffer damage to the left hemisphere, even when they are able to make the movements required.

Suggested Websites for Lecture 16a:

The Corpus Callosum: *http://www.indiana.edu/~pietsch/callosum.html*

From Paul Pietsch's *Shuffle Brain*, an examination of the corpus callosum; great figures, good text, links to related research.

Laterality in Primates: *http://www.indiana.edu/~primate/index.html*

An informative page from M.K. Holder at the University of Indiana on handedness and laterality of function; in particular, see:

http://www.indiana.edu/~primate/brain.html

Nobel Prize and Sperry: *http://www.nobel.se/laureates/medicine-1981.html*

A autobiography for Roger Sperry, celebrating his Nobel Prize "for his discoveries concerning the functional specialization of the cerebral hemispheres".

Two Brains: *http://weber.u.washington.edu/~chudler/split.html*

From Dr. Eric Chudler's excellent site at the University of Washington, a great resource on split brains and laterality of function; good text and figures, and links to related sites on the Web.

Lecture 16b

CORTICAL LOCALIZATION OF LANGUAGE

Outline

1. Broca's Area

2. Wernicke's Area

3. The Wernicke-Geschwind Model

4. Tests of the Wernicke-Geschwind Model
   a. Surgical Lesions
   b. Brain Damage
   c. CAT Scans and MRI Scans
   d. Electrical Stimulation
   e. Dyslexia and Support for a Dual-Route Parellel Model of Reading Aloud
   f. Functional Brain Imaging and the Localization of Language

5. Conclusion

Lecture Notes

1. **Broca's Area** *(use Digital Image Archive Figure CH16F02.BMP)*

   - in 1864, **Broca** hypothesized on the basis of nine postmortem examinations that the inferior portion of the left prefrontal lobe (**Broca's area**) contains programs of articulation; he suggested that Broca's area controls the facial neurons of the **primary motor cortex**
   - the **frontal operculum** is the area of the frontal lobe that is just in front of the face area of the primary motor cortex; in the left hemisphere this is the location of Broca's area; there is more volume of the frontal operculum in the left hemisphere, however associations with language and lateralization should be made cautiously, especially with reference to the frontal operculum

2. **Wernicke's Area**

   - in 1874, Wernicke concluded on the basis of 10 clinical cases that the area in the left temporal lobe just posterior to the **primary auditory cortex** is another important language area; it became known as **Wernicke's area**
   - Wernicke's area was hypothesized by Wernicke to play a role in language comprehension; Wernicke claimed that damage to Broca's area produces **aphasia** that is primarily **expressive**(no deficits in language comprehension and speech that is meaningful, but slow, labored, disjointed, and poorly articulated) and that damage to Wernicke's area produces aphasia that is primarily **receptive** (deficits in language comprehension and speech that has the structure, rhythm, and intonation of real speech but is incomprehensible--a **word salad**)
   - it is important to remember that "**Broca's aphasia**" and "**Wernicke's aphasia**" are predictions of Wernicke, rather than labels of actual disorders
   - Wernicke also argued that damage to the left **arcuate fasciculus**, which connects Broca's and Wernicke's areas, should produce aphasia characterized by a difficulty in repeating words that were heard; he called this third hypothetical form of aphasia **conduction aphasia**
   - the left **planum temporale** (temporal lobe cortex tissue referred to as Wernicke's area) is larger than the right in 65% of people; this may in part explain why language is processed in the left hemisphere for 90% of people; however about 90% of people are left-hemisphere-dominant for language

3. **The Wernicke-Geschwind Model**

- during the era of Broca and Wernicke, the most influential neuroscientists did not favor **localizationist** models, and Broca's and Wernicke's hypotheses had little influence
- however, in 1965 Geschwind combined these ideas with Dejerine's (1892) conclusion that damage in the **angular gyrus** (on the border between the left temporal and parietal lobes, just anterior to the occipital lobe) is the cause of **alexia** and **agraphia**; the model of the cerebral control of language that resulted from Geschwind's synthesis is called the **Wernicke-Geschwind model**
- the Wernicke-Geschwind model is a **serial model**; signals mediating each activity travel between its seven key components in linear sequence (**parallel models** involve two or more routes); *(use Digital Image Archive Figure CH16F10.BMP to illustrate Geschwind's model, and Figure CH16F11.BMP to illustrate how Geschwind proposed it worked)*
- the main support for the model came from Geschwind's interpretation of his own aphasic patients; most of these cases had brain damage that was both diffuse and poorly documented (postmortem confirmation of the lesion site was rarely offered); this is a very weak foundation on which to build a highly localizationist model
- despite the weak foundation of data on which the Wernicke-Geschwind model was built, it has been the dominant neuropsychological theory of language in the quarter century since its publication
- How well has it stood up to the challenge of empirical testing by investigators other than Geschwind?

4. **Tests of the Wernicke-Geschwind Model**

a. **Surgical Lesions**

- in view of the fact that the Wernicke-Geschwind model was developed from the analysis of cases of human brain damage, it is reasonable to ask how well it can account for language-related deficits experienced by patients with brain damage
- patients with surgical lesions are particularly useful for such studies because the site of their lesion is well known; moreover, patients rendered aphasic by accidental brain damage almost always have extensive **subcortical** damage, which leads to widespread degeneration and makes firm **localizationist** interpretations difficult, but this is less of a problem with surgical lesions of the cortex
- several large-scale studies of the language-related deficits experienced by patients with surgical lesions to different areas of the cortex have been conducted; the following are their conclusions:

  1) lesions that destroy Broca's area but little surrounding tissue have no permanent effect on language-related abilities (there are temporary problems that develop a few hours after the operation and disappear in several days, which are presumably the result of **edema**);
  2) discrete lesions that cut through the left arcuate fasciculus or angular gyrus produce no permanent aphasia;
  3) because of the dire predictions of the Wernicke-Geschwind model, Wernicke's area has rarely been totally removed, but there are some cases in which large portions of it have been removed with little permanent effect

- **OVERHEAD T71**; the postsurgical language-related problems experienced by several patients with surgical lesions to the Wernicke-Geschwind areas
- supporters of the Wernicke-Geschwind model discount the data from surgical-lesion studies; they argue that the cortical organization of patients requiring neurosurgery is abnormal

b. Brain Damage *(use Digital Image Archive Figure CH16F14.BMP)*
- several independent studies have assessed the degree to which the Wernicke-Geschwind model can account for the effects of nonsurgical brain damage; this is exactly the type of evidence on which the model was based; the best of these studies have included only cases in which the location of the damage was confirmed by subsequent postmortem examination or visual inspection during surgery
- for example, a study by Hécaen and Angelergues (1964) assessed the performance on several objective tests of speech production, speech comprehension, and reading performed of 214 right-

128

handed patients whose brain damage was located during a subsequent operation or a postmortem examination
- the following were the main findings of Hécaen and Angelergues: (1) lesions restricted to Broca's area seldom produced lasting deficits, whereas those restricted to Wernicke's area sometimes did not; (2) no case was observed that was purely expressive (Broca's aphasia) or purely receptive (Wernicke's aphasia); (3) extremely large (involving three lobes) anterior lesions of the left hemisphere tended to produce more expressive symptoms than receptive symptoms, and the opposite was true of very large posterior lesions; and (4) this same general trend was not observed with less large (involving two lobes) lesions

c. **CAT Scans and MRI Scans**
- since the development of the CAT and MRI, there have been several efforts to correlate aphasic symptoms with brain scan results
- brain scans virtually always reveal extensive cortical and subcortical damage in aphasic patients; aphasia that is more expressive than receptive tends to be associated with large anterior lesions of the left hemisphere, and aphasia that is more receptive than expressive tends to be associated with large posterior lesions
- a few aphasic patients have damage restricted to the medial portions of the frontal lobes
- Damasio (1989) used MRI to confirm earlier CT studies, finding that there were large left hemisphere lesions in almost all situations where language-related abilities were eliminated; however, in a few patients' damage was restricted to the **medial frontal lobes** and the **anterior cingulate cortex**, areas not implicated in language according to the Wernicke-Geschwind model.
- Alexander (1989) used CT and MRI to show that aphasia can result from damage to subcortical structures
- Naeser et al., (1982) found aphasia following damage to the left subcortical white matter, the left **basal ganglia**, or the left **thalamus**

d. **Electrical Stimulation**
- in the 1940s, Penfield and his colleagues were the first to stimulate the brains of conscious human patients during brain surgery; at some sites the stimulation disrupted various speech-related activities; this suggested that brain stimulation might be a valuable method for mapping the language areas of the cortex; stimulation produces a much more local disruption than a brain lesion
- in 1959, Penfield and Roberts reported the results obtained from over 10 years of research; they determined sites at which stimulation (1) rendered the patient mute, (2) disturbed articulation, (3) caused the patient to make counting errors, (4) interfered with the patient's ability to name objects, or (5) caused the patient to misname objects
- Penfield and Roberts found that: (1) aphasia-like responses to right-hemisphere stimulation were rare, (2) each deficit was produced by stimulation of sites **scattered** throughout much of the left hemisphere, (3) there was no apparent tendency for the stimulation of Broca's area to produce deficits different from those produced by stimulation of Wernicke's area
- Ojemann (1983) assessed naming, reading of simple sentences, short-term verbal memory, ability to mimic orofacial movements, and the ability to recognize **phonemes** (units of sound) during cortical stimulation; it was found that (1) sites at which stimulation could disrupt language extended beyond the Wernicke-Geschwind language areas, (2) all of the specific language abilities were represented in anterior and posterior sites, and
(3) there were major differences across subjects in the organization of language abilities
- Mateer and Cameron (1989) used cortical stimulation, finding that the cortex around the lateral fissure was specifically organized for **phonologocal analysis** (sound analysis) and other cortical speech areas dealt with **grammatical analysis** (structure of language) and **semantic analysis** (meaning of language)

e. **Dyslexia and Support for a Dual-Route Parellel Model of Reading Aloud**
- **dyslexia** is an inability to read or write despite normal or superior intelligence; this disorder is common, affecting about 15% of males and about 5% of females.
- research in the area has suggested a **dual-route parallel model** of language, in which two types of processing of the same input occur over two different neural pathways.
- the first path is a lexical system (based on stored information about the pronunciation of specific words); and the second system is a nonlexical system (based on stored abstractions or rules of pronunciation)

- evidence for the duality of the neural pathways mediating these two different ways of processing language come from dyslexics, who may be deficit in just one of the two areas. For example in **surface dyslexia** patients pronounce words or nonsense words according to the nonlexical system (i.e., "have" and "steak" are pronounced to rhyme with "cave" and "teak"); in contrast, patients with **deep dyslexia** to the overall look, meaning, or derivation of the word but can't apply the nonlexical system ("quill" for quail," "wise" for "wisdom," or "hen" for "chicken")
- Coltheart (1980) has suggested that the neural mechanisms underlying the nonlexical type of analyses are lateralized to the left hemisphere. This idea is supported by a patient who had a left **hemispherectomy**; this patient could speak familiar concrete words but could not pronounce simple nonwords, and her errors suggested that she was reading based on the meaning and appearance of words rather than translating their letters into sounds.

f. **Functional Brain Imaging and the Localization of Language**
- Petersen et al., (1989) PET and the **paired image subtraction technique** to study the localization of language in the brain
- in their experiment, there were four visual conditions of gradually increasing complexity: (1) fixate on a point, 2) fixate while printed nouns appear, (3) fixate and read the nouns aloud, and (4) fixate and say a verb associated with a noun.
- there were also four comparable auditory conditions
- three subtractions were performed in which a given scan was subtracted from the scan that followed it, on both the auditory and the visual versions of the test, for each of the four conditions. For example, the activity in condition 1 was subtracted from the activity in condition 2 to assess the activity associated with silent reading (or hearing) the nouns
- the results were inconsistent with the Wernicke-Geschwind model in several ways *(use Digital Image Archive Figure CH16F14.BMP)*:

  (1) the presentation of printed verbs added activity to secondary cortex in **both hemispheres**;
  (2) speaking the nouns aloud added activity in the **somatosensory** and **motor cortices** of **both hemispheres** and in the **lateral fissure** of the right hemisphere; and
  (3) the verb-association condition always added activity in the **medial frontal cortex** of both hemispheres and to an area just in front of Broca's area in the left hemisphere

- based on their research, Peterseon and his colleagues have proposed a dual-route theory of language processing. When subjects engage in a well-practiced verbal response, processing moves from sensory areas to the motor areas via association cortices in the lateral fissure. However, when subjects engage in a more complex response, information flows from the sensory cortices to association cortices in the frontal and cingulate areas.

5. Conclusion

- if, on the basis of the overwhelmingly negative evidence, you conclude that the Wernicke-Geschwind model has not been an important theory, you would be missing an important point
- the purpose of a scientific theory is to stimulate and direct research and to provide a context for its interpretation
- the Wernicke-Geshwind model has served these functions admirably; it has stimulated and directed research on the neuropsychology of language for a quarter century

Suggested Websites for Lecture 16b:

Dyslexia: *http://www.sciam.com/1196issue/1196shaywitz.html*

From Scientific American, a review of the neural bases of dyslexia

Conversation's With Neil's Brain: *http://williamcalvin.com/bk7/bk7.htm*

Lecture 17a

BIOPSYCHOLOGY OF EMOTION AND STRESS

Outline

1. Early Research on the Biopsychology of Emotion
    a. Darwin
    b. James-Lange and Cannon-Bard Theories
    c. Sham Rage, the Limbic System, and Kulver-Bucy Syndrome

2. Human Facial Expressions of Emotion
    a. The Primary Facial Expressions
    b. Facial Feedback Hypothesis
    c. Deceptive Facial Expressions

3. Cortical Mechanisms of Emotion

4. Fear, Defense, and Aggression

5. Neural Mechanisms of Fear and Conditioned Fear

Lecture Notes

1. **Early Research on the Biopsychology of Emotion**

    a. **Darwin**
        - Darwin's **The Expression of Emotions in Man and Animals** was the first major event in the study of the biopsychological bases of emotion.
        - Darwin believed that emotions evolved from behaviors that indicated what an animal would do next in a given situation; that when these behaviors were advantageous to the animal (e.g., allowed it to avoid a fight), they evolved in a way that would enhance their communicative value, to the extent that the original behavior was lost; and that opposite messages are signalled by opposite types of behaviors (**the principle of antithesis,** *use Digital Image Archive Figure CH17F01.BMP)*

    b. **James-Lange and Cannon-Bard Theories of Emotion** *(use Digital Image Archive Figure CH17F02.BMP)*
        - the James-Lange theory was the first attempt to explain the physiological bases of emotion; in their theory, James and Lange suggested that emotion-inducing stimuli are received and interpreted by the brain, which triggers visceral changes that subsequently trigger the experience of emotion.
        - Cannon, and subsequently Bard, proposed an alternative theory based on the idea that emotional stimuli evoke a viseral and an emotional response response that were independent of one another
        - it appears that neither theory was entirely correct; emotions can be induced by stimuli that cannot elicit a peripheral, visceral response (e.g., in patients suffering from a spinal cord transection), but visceral responses can often induce an emotional state in the absence of any obvious eliciting stimuli (e.g., a racing heartbeat and increased respiration can produce a feeling of fear in the absence of an eliciting stimuli).

    c. **Sham Rage, the Limbic System, and the Kulver-Bucy Syndrome**
        - in 1929, Bard reported that cats that had been **decorticated** (their cerebral cortex was removed) responded with unusual aggression to the slightest provocation; often, this behavior was not even directed at any specific topic. Bard concluded that the hypothalamus is critical for the performance of aggressive behaviors, and that the cortex normally inhibited and directed these aggressive displays.

- this theory of hypothalamic function was followed by Papez's proposal of a **limbic system** *(use Digital Image Archive Figure CH17F03.BMP)* that controlled the expression of emotions by connections with the hypothalamus and mediated the perception of emotions by connections with the cortex.
- this idea was supported in part by the observation that damage to a part of the limbic system…specifically, to the amygdala, would produce a syndrome in which a subject was fearless, hypersexual, and inclined to explore objects with their mouths. This was called the Kluver-Bucy syndrome, after the investigators who first reported it

2. Human Facial Expressions of Emotion

a. The Primary Facial Expressions
- much of the classic research on human facial expressions has been conducted by Ekman and Friesen beginning in the 1970s; they began by analyzing hundreds of films and photographs of people experiencing various emotions; they concluded that there are six primary facial expressions of emotion and that all other expressions were mixtures of these; the six primary expressions were expressions of: (1) **anger,** (2) **fear,** (3) **happiness,** (4) **surprise,** (5) **sadness,** and (6) **disgust**
- Darwin had earlier proposed that facial expressions are universal to the human species; this hypothesis was tested by showing people from 12 different cultures facial expressions from Ekman and Friesen's atlas; the photographs were of people who had been instructed to contract specific facial muscles (e.g., to make a surprised expression, the models were instructed to pull their eyebrows upward so as to wrinkle their forehead, to open their eyes wide to reveal white above the iris, to slacken the muscles around the mouth, and to drop the jaw)
- the people from all 12 cultures linked the same emotions to the facial expressions, thus supporting Darwin's hypothesis. In addition, Ekman and Friesen found that isolated New Guinea tribe members could correctly identify Western facial expressions and that Westerners could correctly identify New Guinean expressions, further supporting the idea of the universality of emotions

b. Facial Feedback Hypothesis of Emotions
- recall that, according to the James-Lange theory of emotion, the body first produces a visceral, peripheral response to emotional stimuli, and then the feeling of emotion comes from the body's perception of its own reactions; although it is now clear that feedback from the body's reactions is not necessary to feel emotion, the question remains, "Can the expression of emotion influence the feeling of emotion?"
- one version of this hypothesis focuses on the idea that facial expression can influence emotional experience. This is called the **facial feedback hypothesis**; Can putting on a happy face make you feel better?
- the answer seems to be yes; Rutledge and Hupka (1985) asked subjects to hold various facial poses while they viewed slides; the subjects reported slightly more happy when making happy faces, and slightly more angry when making angry faces
- try this: pull your eyebrows down and together, raise your upper eyelids, tighten your lower eyelids, narrow your lips and press them together; if holding this expression of anger makes you feel slightly uneasy you have experienced the facial feedback hypothesis

c. Deceptive Facial Expressions
- because we can exert voluntary control over the facial muscles, we can inhibit true facial expressions and substitute false ones; there are positive and negative reasons for this
- it is difficult to fool an expert because microexpressions of the genuine emotion often break through the false one; although they are usually very short (about .05 seconds), they can often be spotted by an expert even without slow-motion analysis
- also, there tend to be subtle differences between genuine and false expressions that can be recognized by an expert; for example, **Duchenne** a French neuroanatomist pointed out in 1862 that genuine smiles (which have been known as **Duchenne smiles**) involve contraction of both the **zygomaticus major** and **orbicularis oculi**, whereas false smiles involve only the zygomaticus major

3. Cortical Mechanisms of Emotion

- in general, the **prefrontal cortex** is associated with emotions; recall that prefrontal lobotomy produced a general emotional blunting. In addition, the **right hemisphere** seems to be more involved with emotion than the left hemisphere: right hemisphere lesions tend to disrupt the perception of facial expression and the emotional tone of speech (**prosody**) more than left hemisphere lesions
- Kolb and his colleagues (1988) found that frontal lobe lesions, **regardless of side**, resulted in fewer facial expressions

4. Fear, Defense and Aggression

- **fear** is the emotional reaction to threat; **defensive behaviors** are intended to protect an animal from threat, while **aggressive behaviors** are intended to threaten or harm.
- ethoexperimental research on emotional expression in nonhuman species has focused on aggression and defense, primarily in rats
- two important concepts have emerged from this study:

   (1) neither aggression or defense are unitary concepts; there are different kinds of aggression and defense, which occur in **different situations**, have a **different topography**, and have a **different neural basis**;
   (2) many of the complexities of aggressive and defensive behavior can be understood in terms of the concept of **target sites**, the idea that different kinds of aggression tend to be directed at particular sites on the defender's body and that various defensive maneuvers appear to be specifically designed to protect these sites

- **social aggression** is unprovoked aggression against a conspecific for the purpose of establishing, maintaining, or altering a social hierarchy; in many mammals it occurs only among males; unlike other forms of aggression, it is dependent on testosterone in many species
- the Blanchard's have fruitfully studied social aggression using the **colony-intruder model**; a small male **intruder** is placed in an established colony, and the interaction between the intruder and the **alpha male** is studied
- social aggression by the alpha male is characterized by **piloerection, lateral attack**, bites directed at the back near the base of the tail, and movements that get the alpha male in position to deliver such bites; the alpha male will not bite any other part of the intruder
- the defensive behavior that is displayed by the intruder includes **flight, freezing** when cornered, **boxing** and pivoting to keep the alpha male away from its back, lying on its back, and, when pressed, **defensive attack** (a lunging biting attack directed at the alpha male's head)
- the discovery that aggressive and defensive behaviors occur in a variety of **stereotypical, species-specific forms** allowed a more clear understanding of the neural bases for these behaviors; for example, the **lateral septum** was once thought to inhibit all aggression because lesions there rendered laboratory rats very difficult to handle; we now know that these lesions actually increase defensive reactivity and predatory aggression while they decrease social aggression.

5. Neural Mechanisms of Fear and Conditioned Fear

- three lines of evidence implicate the **amygdala** as playing a key role in the experience and expression of fear. This evidence has all arisen out of the study of **conditioned fear**. In one example of this type of study, the subject (usually a rat) hears a tone that signals a mild electric shock. After several pairings, the tone elicits defensive behaviors and autonomic responses associated with the shock itself. LeDoux and his colleagues have mapped the neural systems that underlie this form of **auditory fear conditioning**
- LeDoux found that lesions to the **medial geniculate nucleus** of the thalamus blocked fear conditioning, but lesions to **primary auditory cortex** did not. This suggested that an alternate neural structure was involved in the fear conditioning; this turned out to be the amygdala, as lesions there also blocked the auditory fear conditioning. Pathways from the amygdala to the **periaqueductal gray** have been found

to mediate many defensive behaviors; pathways to the lateral hypothalamus elicit the appropriate sympathetic responses.

interestingly, there is a second pathway from the medial geniculate nucleus of the thalamus to the amygdala that passes through primary auditory cortex; if either the direct or the indirect route is intact, fear conditioning can occur.

Suggested Websites for Lecture 17a:

The Emotional Brain: *http://www.latimes.com/HOME/NEWS/SCIENCE/REPORTS/THEBRAIN/emote.htm*

From the Los Angeles Times's *The Brain* site, a review on new imaging techniques and the neural substrates of emotion; good text, though sadly no figures.

The Limbic System: *http://www.epub.org.br/cm/n05/mente/limbic_i.htm*

From the Brain and Mind site, a review of the limbic system and its role in emotion.

Neural Bases of Fear: *http://thalamus.wustl.edu/course/limbic.html*

Fear and the limbic system, from Washington University's Neuroscience tutorial page. You will have to scroll down the page to find this section; brief text, good figures.

Lecture 17b

STRESS AND PSYCHOSOMATIC DISORDERS

Outline

1. The Stress Response

2. Stress and Ulcers

3. Psychoneuroimmunology: Stress and Infection

4. Stress and the Hippocampus

Lecture Notes

1. **The Stress Response**

    -   **Selye** first described the stress response in the 1950's; he identified several physiological responses to stress, emphasizing the role of the **anterior pituitary-adrenal cortex system** and the effects of stress on the release of ACTH, and glucocorticoids. He also recognized the **dual nature** of stress: **acute stress** elicited adaptive changes that allowed an organism to cope with the stressor, but **chronic stress** produced changes that were maladaptive
    -   recent research has also implicated the importance of the sympathetic nervous system's release of **epinephrine** and **norepinephrine** in the response to stress
    -   McEwen (1994) hypothesized that the magnitude of the stress response was dependent upon 3 factors: the **stressor**, the **individual**, and **strategies to cope** with stress
    -   Selye's work remains important to the psychological sciences because it provided a link through which psychological factors might impact upon physical illness. **Psychosomatic illnesses** are ones that have a physical basis that is greatly influenced by psychological factors. Two examples of psychosomatic illness include **ulcers** and **infection.**

2. **Stress and Ulcers**

    -   **gastric ulcers** are painful lesions to the lining of the stomach and small intestine; stress has been implicated in their development, with the key factor being a stress-induced increase in acidic gastric secretions accompanied by decreased blood flow through the wall of the stomach.
    -   recent evidence has suggested that the bacteria *Helicobacter pylori* are responsible for all ulcers except by those caused by nonsteroidal anti-inflammatory drugs. However, it seems as though *H. pylori* by itself is not sufficient to induce the formation of ulcers, as it is found in about 75% of all control subjects, too. Currently, researchers believe that stress-induced increases in gastric secretions and decreases in blood flow interact with *H. pylori* to produce ulcers.

3. **Psychoneuroimmunology: Stress and Infection**

    -   **psychoneuroimmunology** is the study of interactions among psychological, nervous system, and immune system responses allows a theoretical basis for studying a person's resistance to disease and infection
    -   the **immune system** puts up barriers to keep the body from being taken over by invading microorganisms
    -   **phagocytosis** is a nonspecific mechanism by which foreign microorganisms are destroyed; this process is carried out by **macrophages**

- there is also a second, more specific mechanism for dealing with foreign microorganisms and debris
- **antigens** are protein molecules on a cell's surface that identify it as foreign or native
- **lymphocytes** are specialized white blood cells, produced in the bone marrow, and stored in the lymphatic system; there are two types of lymphocytes, that each mediate a form of immunological defense:

   1) **T cells** are lymphocytes that destroy invading microorganisms in a process called cell-**mediated immunity**; and
   2) **B cells** are lymphocytes that manufacture **antibodies** (lethal receptor molecules) against antigens encountered on foreign cells and debris, in a process called **antibody-mediated immunity**

- in humans, stress from sources such as final examinations, sleep deprivation, divorce, bereavement etc., has been shown to decrease the effectiveness of the immune system. Unfortunately, these results are not straightforward to interpret as there are many possible **confounds**; for example, stressed subjects may report more illnesses because they expect to be ill, the experience of illness may be worse under stress, or stress may cause illness-inducing behavioral changes rather than the illness itself (e.g., decreases in sleep; alterations in diet)
- in support of these human findings, similar results have been seen in laboratory animals exposed to electric shocks, social defeat, overcrowding etc. Together, these converging lines of data suggest that stress may play a major role in our susceptibility to many infectious diseases.
- stress may affect the immune system by affecting **hormonal activity** mediated through the anterior pituitary-adrenal cortex system and the sympathetic adrenal medulla system; for example, both T-cells and B-cells have receptors for glucocorticoids and for norepinephrine and epinephrine, which are all released in very high levels during periods of stress

4. **Stress and the Hippocampus**

- it has been demonstrated that **early handling** of rat pups reduces the glucocorticoid levels observed in these animals as adults; this is an intriguing finding, as glucocorticoids have been linked to many adverse effects including neural cell loss with aging.
- subsequent studies revealed decrease cell loss in the **hippocampus** of rats that were handled as pups, accompanied by **fewer memory deficits** associated with aging.
- in truth, the handling was not critical to this effect, as it was later discovered that the handled pups received more maternal attention than unhandled controls; however, it did provide an interesting link between early experience, stress, and the function of the nervous system.
- these findings became even more important when it was discovered that the **dentate gyrus** of the hippocampus of rats, unlike any known other cell in the central nervous system, continue to be produced throughout the lifespan of an individual. Stress or elevated levels of glucocorticoids block the creation of these new cells, which may account for the hippocampal cell damage that is observed in animals that have been chronically stressed.

Suggested Websites for Chapter 17b:

Stress and Pychosomatic Disorders: *http://www.epub.org.br/cm/n03/doencas/stress_i.htm*

A look at stress and its effects on general health, from the Brain and Mind site.

THE BIOPSYCHOLOGY OF SCHIZOPHRENIA, AFFECTIVE DISORDERS and ANXIETY

Outline

1. Schizophrenia
   a) The First Antischizophrenic Drugs
   b) Dopamine Theory of Schizophrenia
   c) The Dopamine Theory: Unanswered Questions

2. Affective Disorders
   a) Symptoms and Etiology
   b) Antidepressant Drugs
   c) Monoamine Theory of Depression
   d) Hypothalamic-Pituitary-Adrenal Theory of Depression
   e) Diathesis-Stress Model of Depression
   f) Neural Mechanisms of Depression: Unanswered Questions

3. Anxiety Disorders

Lecture Notes

1. Schizophrenia

- **schizophrenia** literally means a splitting of psychic function ("the shattered mind"); it is characterized by a complex and diverse set of symptoms that often overlap with other forms of mental illness and may change with time
- individuals with any of the following symptoms are diagnosed as schizophrenic: **bizarre delusions**, **hallucinations**, **inappropriate affect**, **incoherent thought**, or **odd behavior** (e.g., **catatonia**)
- about 1% of the population is schizophrenic; another 2 or 3% display marginal symptoms; the incidence appears to be about the same in all parts of the world
- a genetic basis for the disease emerged when it was recognized that the concordance rate of schizophrenia in identical twins is about 45%; in fraternal twins it is about 10%
- in addition to a genetic predisposition, experiences such as **prenatal trauma**, **infection**, and **stress** may all be susceptibility factors
- clearly schizophrenia is influenced by both genetics and experience

a) The First Antischizophrenic Drugs

- **chlorpromazine** was initially developed by a drug company as a new **antihistamine** in 1950, a French physician wrote the company because he was trying to find an antihistamine that would prevent the swelling associated with surgery; they sent him a few that were in the developmental stages, including chlorpromazine; he tried them and by chance noticed that chlorpromazine, although not an effective antihistamine, seemed to calm his patients down
- the French physician recommended that his psychiatrist colleagues try it as a **sedative** in difficult-to-manage psychiatric cases; in most cases it didn't seem to work; however, one of the psychiatrists administered large doses of chlorpromazine for several weeks, and he noticed a marked improvement in several **schizophrenic** patients after 3 weeks
- amazingly the chlorpromazine seemed to calm agitated schizophrenic patients and to activate catatonic ones; therefore the effect seemed specifically antischizophrenic, not just **sedative** (sleep-inducing)
- also in the early 1950s, an American psychiatrist became interested in reports that the **snake root plant** had been used for centuries in India as a cure for various psychiatric disturbances

- **reserpine**, the active ingredient of the snakeroot plant, had been isolated so he gave it to some of his schizophrenic patients
- it proved to be an effective antischizophrenic; however, it is no longer used for treatment of schizophrenia due to its effects of dangerously lowering blood pressure

b) Dopamine Theory of Schizophrenia

- given the dissimilarity of the structure of chlorpromazine and reserpine, the similarity of their effects was remarkable; their therapeutic effects did not occur until 2 or 3 weeks after the beginning of therapy, and at that time both drugs started to produce side effects; mild tremors that were most obvious when the patient was inactive, muscular rigidity, and a decrease in voluntary movement
- you should recognize these symptoms as the symptoms of **Parkinson's disease**; it seemed that the same neurochemical changes that were the basis of these drugs' antischizophrenic action were inducing the Parkinson's symptoms
- in 1960, it was discovered that there was a deficiency of **dopamine** in the brains of Parkinson's patients; thus it seemed that both chlorpromazine and reserpine reduced brain dopamine levels and that this reduction was alleviating the symptoms of schizophrenia; on the basis of these two inferences it was proposed that schizophrenia is associated with excessive activity in dopaminergic systems in the brain
- two previous findings lent support to this theory:

    (1) reserpine was known to be a **dopamine antagonist** (it depleted the brain of dopamine and other monoamines by causing them to leak from their vesicles); and
    (2) stimulants, which are agonists of dopamine and other monoamines, trigger schizophrenic episodes in healthy subjects at high doses (e.g., **amphetamine psychosis**)

- in 1963, **Carlsson** and **Lindqvist** tested the dopamine theory; they expected to show that chlorpromazine, like reserpine, depletes the brain of dopamine--but they didn't; they found instead that chlorpromazine left dopamine levels unchanged, but that it produced a great increase in dopamine **metabolites**
- they concluded that, like reserpine, chlorpromazine is a **dopamine antagonist**, but that it antagonizes dopamine in a different way
- they suggested that chlorpromazine is a **false transmitter** at dopamine synapses; that a **feedback signal** produced by the inactivity of the postsynaptic neurons causes the presynaptic neurons to release more dopamine; that this excess of dopamine is immediately broken down by enzymes in the synapse because all of the binding sites are taken up by chlorpromazine; and that as a result dopamine levels stay about the same but metabolite levels increase
- a technique developed in the mid 1970s allowed Snyder and his colleagues to measure the degree to which various antischizophrenic drugs bind to dopamine receptors, and to relate this **binding affinity** to the potency with which each drug alleviated schizophrenic symptoms in human patients
- the correlation was positive, but there were some disturbing exceptions; for example, **haloperidol**, one of the most potent antischizophrenic drugs, bound only weakly to dopamine receptors
- the answer to this puzzle was suggested by the discovery that there are **two dopamine receptor subtypes:** D_1 and D_2
- it turned out that chlorpromazine and all other antischizophrenic drugs of the same chemical class (i.e., the **phenothiazines**) bind with equal affinity to both D_1 and D_2 receptors; in contrast, haloperidol and the other **butyrophenones** bind with highest affinity to D_2 receptors
- this suggested a modification to the dopamine theory of schizophrenia, as schizophrenia could now be viewed as being caused by excess activity at D_2 receptors and alleviated by drugs that block activity at D_2 receptors *(use Digital Image Archive Figure CH17F14.BMP)*

c) The Dopamine Theory of Schizophrenia: Unanswered Questions

- there are still five questions about the dopamine theory of schizophrenia that have yet to be resolved:

    1) Why is **clozapine**, an atypical neuroleptic that binds poorly to D_2 receptors, effective against schizophrenia? The discovery of new dopamine receptors provides the possible answer; clozapine and conventional neuroleptics bind to D1 and D4 receptors and some **serotonin** receptors; perhaps these are critical receptors in schizophrenia.

2) Why does it take 2 or 3 weeks for antischizophrenic drugs to take effect when they block receptors almost immediately? It appears that the therapeutic effect of blockade is mediated by neural adaptation (slow developing compensatory changes) to the blockade rather than by the blockade. One hypothesis is that prolongued neuroleptic treatment eventually produces **depolarization blockade** in dopamine neurons, and it is this decrease in activity that is related to the drug's therapeutic effect.

3) What brain regions are involved in schizophrenia? Imaging studies have revealed many changes, including small cerebral cortices and large ventricles. To date, no pathology in brain dopaminergic systems has been reported.

4) Why do antischizophrenic drugs help only some patients? The current hypothesis is that cases dominated by **positive symptoms** (hallucinations, delusions, incoherence) are caused by excess dopamine activity and are helped; those cases dominated by **negative symptoms** (catatonia, blunt affect, poverty of speech) have brain damage and are not helped.

5) In what way does stress activate schizophrenic symptoms? One possibility is that stress activation of dopaminergic projections to the prefrontal cortex areas that may have abnormal development in schizophrenics

2. Affective Disorders

a) Symptoms and Etiology
- all of us have experienced depression; people in whom depression is so severe and so frequent, often without obvious cause, are said to be suffering from the psychiatric disorder of **depression**; depression can be **reactive** (triggered by negative experiences) or **endogenous,** (no apparent external triggers)
- 40% of clinically depressed people also experience periods of mania (talkative, energetic, impulsive, confident, distractible, unrealistic); these people are said to suffer from **bipolar affective disorder**; the 60% of depressed people who do not experience periods of mania are said to suffer from **unipolar affective disorder**
- about 6% of people suffer from unipolar affective disorder and 1% from bipolar affective disorder at some point in their lives
- the **concordance rate** of bipolar affective disorder for identical twins is about 60%; for fraternal twins it is about 15%; thus, there is a strong genetic component
- like schizophrenia, **stress** plays a major role in the etiology of affective disorders; stress can trigger attacks of depression, and there is some indication that early exposure to stress increases the likelihood of developing depression in adulthood

b. Antidepressant Drugs
- the first antidepressant drug, **iproniazid,** was developed as a treatment for tuberculosis; it had no effect on tuberculosis, but it did leave the patients less depressed about their condition and its clinical usefulness in this regard was soon exploited
- iproniazid is an **MAO inhibitor**; MAO inhibitors are no longer used for depression because they block the metabolism of **tyramine** by the liver; MAO inhibitors in combination with tyramine-rich foods (e.g., cheese, wine, or pickles) cause life-threatening surges in blood pressure; this is called the **cheese effect**
- **imipramine,** the first **tricyclic antidepressant**, was initially developed as an antischizophrenic drug; when it was tried on a mixed group of psychiatric patients, it was found to be ineffective against schizophrenia but affective against depression
- **lithium chloride** is affective against mania as well as depression; it was discovered when an Australian psychiatrist attempted to induce experimental mania in guinea pigs by injecting the urine of manic patients, mixed with lithium chloride to form an injectable salt; the guinea pigs became very inactive, even those in the lithium-chloride control group; thus, he concluded that lithium had calmed the guinea pigs; he was wrong, the lithium merely made them ill; nevertheless, this study encouraged some clinical trials; it was found to be effective against both mania and depression and today is the treatment of choice for bipolar affective disorder

- **Prozac,** a selective **serotonin-selective reuptake inhibitor**, is a variation of tricyclic antidepressants which selectively blocks serotonin uptake *(use Digital Image Archive Figure CH17F14.BMP).* It is not more effective than imipramine against depression but it has fewer side effects and has benefited those with forms of depression expressed in a lack of self esteem, fear of failure etc.

c) Monoamine Theory of Depression

- MAO inhibitors are monoamine **agonists**; all clinically effective tricyclic antidepressants are serotonin and norepinephrine agonists, they **block reuptake** from synapses
- thus, it was suggested that depression is caused by underactivity at serotonin and norepinephrine synapses; there is evidence that certain norepinephrine and serotonin receptors are elevated in untreated depressed patients.

d) Hypothalamic-Pituitary-Adrenal Theory of Depression

- this is based on the observation that depressed patients synthesize more **corticotrophin-releasing hormone** from their hypothalamus, which causes a greater release of **adrenocorticotropic hormone** from the anterior pituitary, which caused increased **glucocorticoid** release from the adrenal cortex. The elevated glucocorticoid levels may play a role in the development of depression, an idea supported by the fact that injections of corticotrophin-releasing hormone can induce signs of depression.

e) Diathesis-Stress Model of Depression

- this theory is based on the idea that some people inherit a predisposition for depression—possibly because of insufficient monaminergic neurotransmission, or because of their hypothalamic-pituitary-adrenal axis is hyperactive, or because of both sets of neural dysfunctions.
- this predisposition is not itself sufficient for the development of depression; however, if the individual is stressed early in life their systems become altered so that they are hypersensitive to stress for the rest of their lives. This leads to the development of depression.

f) Neural Mechanisms of Depression: Unanswered Questions

- there are many questions still left about the neural bases of affective disorders; here are 4 of them:

   1) Why does it take weeks for antidepressant drugs to be clinically effective? This suggests that it is some slow-developing response to elevated monoamine levels, rather than the elevated transmitter levels themselves, that produce the antidepressant effeect.
   2) How do antidepressant drugs that do not directly affect monoaminergic systems elicit their antidepressant effect?
   3) Why do some monoamine agonists (the notable examples being cocaine and amphetamine) not produce antidepressant effects?
   4) How does sleep deprivation induce its antidepressant effect?

3. Anxiety Disorders

- **Anxiety** is a fear that disrupts normal functioning and persists in the absence of a direct threat; these are the most prevalent of all psychiactric disorders; there are four major classes of anxiety:

   - **generalized anxiety** is a stress response in the absence of an obvious stimulus
   - **phobic anxiety** is caused by exposure to a specific object or   situation (snakes, height etc.)
   - **panic disorders** are rapid onset attacks characterized by extreme fear and stress symptoms (tachycardia, choking etc.)
   - **obsessive-compulsive disorders** are frequently recurring, uncontrollable anxiety-producing thoughts and compensatory responses

- treatment often includes **benzodiazepines** (Librium, Valium) that increase the binding of GABA to the receptor; problematic side effects include tremors, nausea, and addiction;

140

- the efficacy of the new anxiolytic **buspirone**, which is an agonist at serotonin type 1-A receptors, suggests that serotonergic systems may also be involved in anxiety
- attention is being focused on brain structures such as the **amygdala**, due to the role that the amygdala plays in conditional fear, the amygdala's high concentration of GABAA receptors, and the fact that local infusions of benzodiazepines into the amygdala-producing anxiolytic effects in animals, and demonstrations that local injections of GABA antagonists into the amygdala can block the anxiolytic effects of systemic injections of benzodiazepines

Suggested Websites for Lecture 17c:

Anxiety Disorders: *http://anxiety.mentalhelp.net/*

A page briefly explaining the symptoms and treatment of anxiety, with links to related sites.

National Anxiety Foundation: *http://lexington-on-line.com/naf.html*

Home page for the National Anxiety Foundation; information on anxiety, panic attacks, OCD.

Neural Bases of Depression: *http://www.sciam.com/1998/0698issue/0698nemeroff.html*

From Scientific American, an article by Dr. Charles Nemeroff on the neural bases of depression; includes information about norepinephrine, serotonin, corticotropin-releasing hormone and the contribution of new imagin techniques in the study of depression.

Shock Therapy: *http://www.epub.org.br/cm/n04/historia/shock_i.htm*

From the Brain and Mind site and the State University of Campinas in Brazil, an examination of the role of ECT, insulin shock, convulsions and other forms of "shock therapy"; interesting historical overview of a controversial topic.

The Discovery of Antipsychotics: *http://www.pbs.org/wgbh/aso/databank/entries/dh52dr.html*

From the Public Broadcasting System's A Science Odyssey, a description of Laborit's discovery of chlorpromazine.

Mental Illness: *http://www.latimes.com/HOME/NEWS/SCIENCE/REPORTS/THEBRAIN/mental.htm*

Another good page from the LA Times' The Brain site, looking at current thought on schizophrenia.